Coloring book

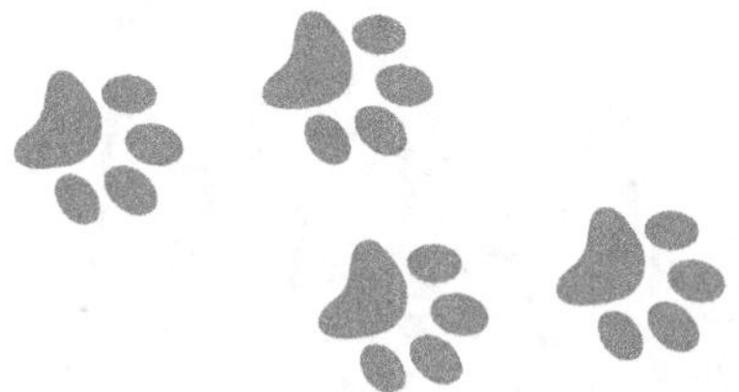

LITTLE PAWS

By

Sergio Iker

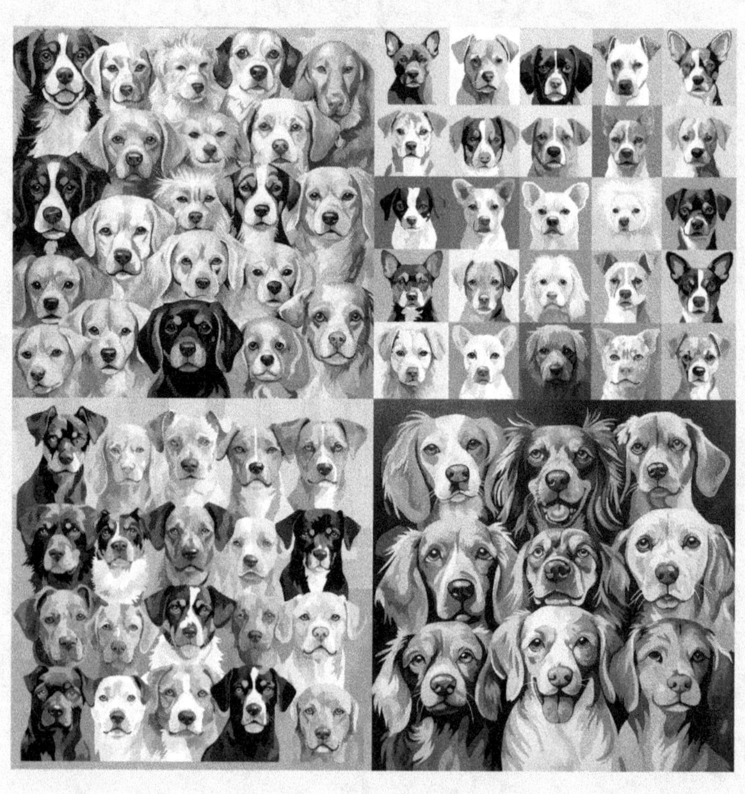

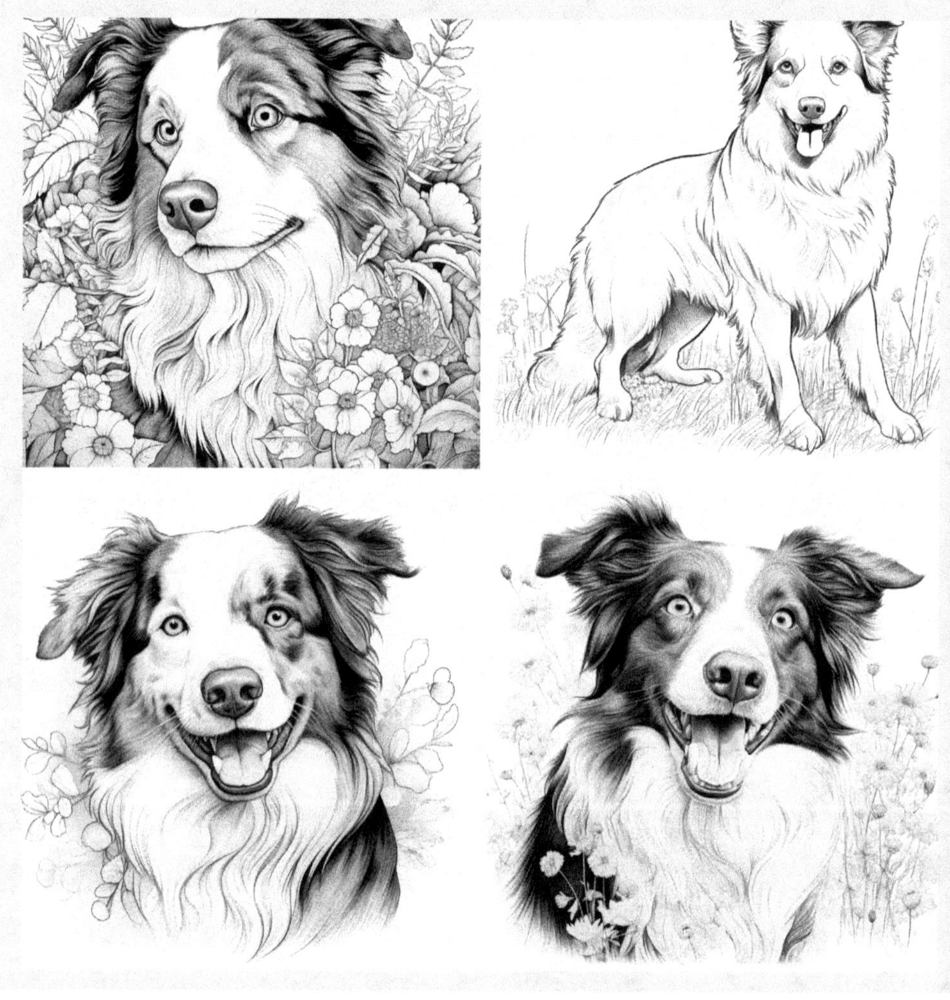

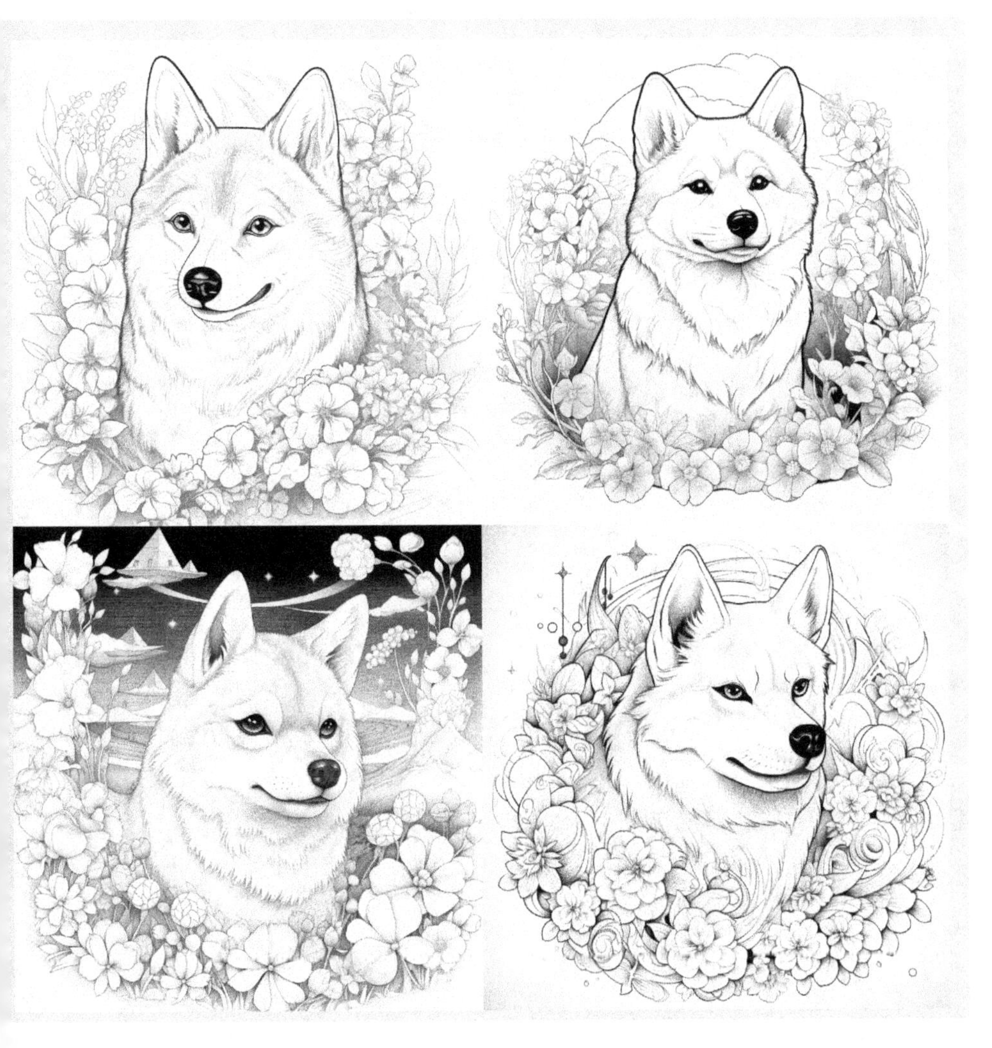

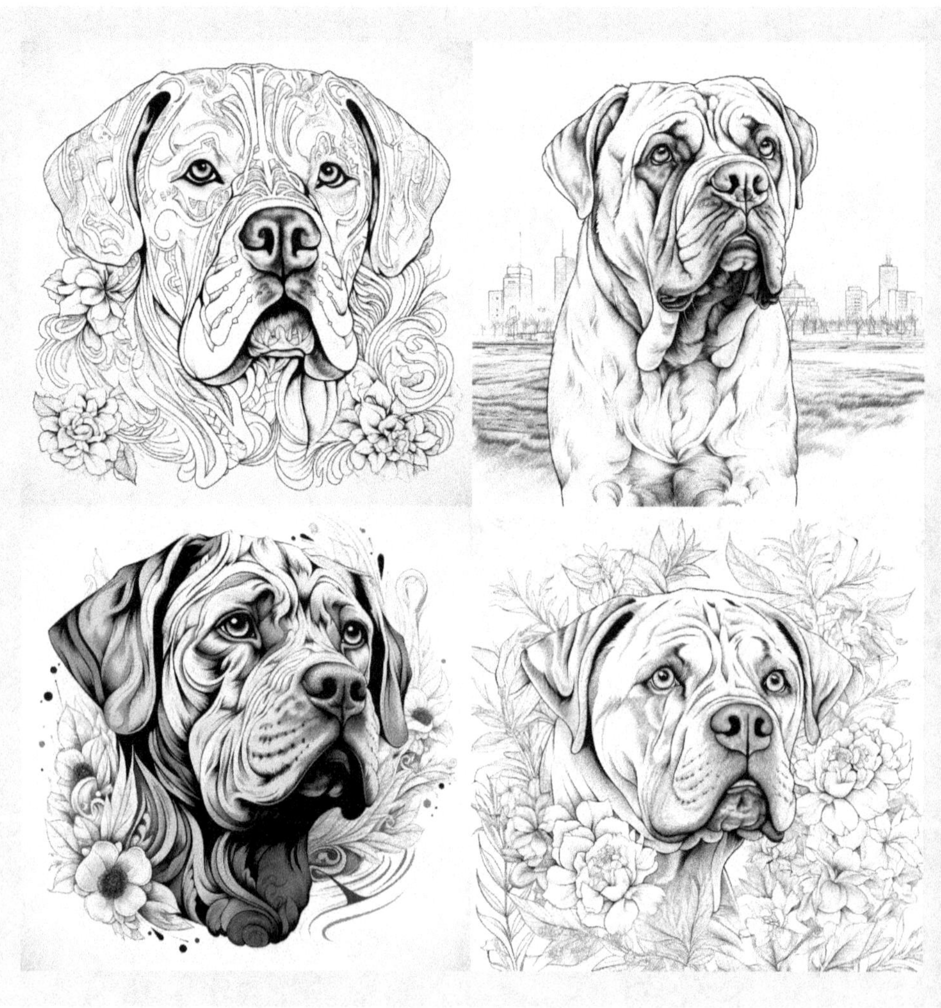

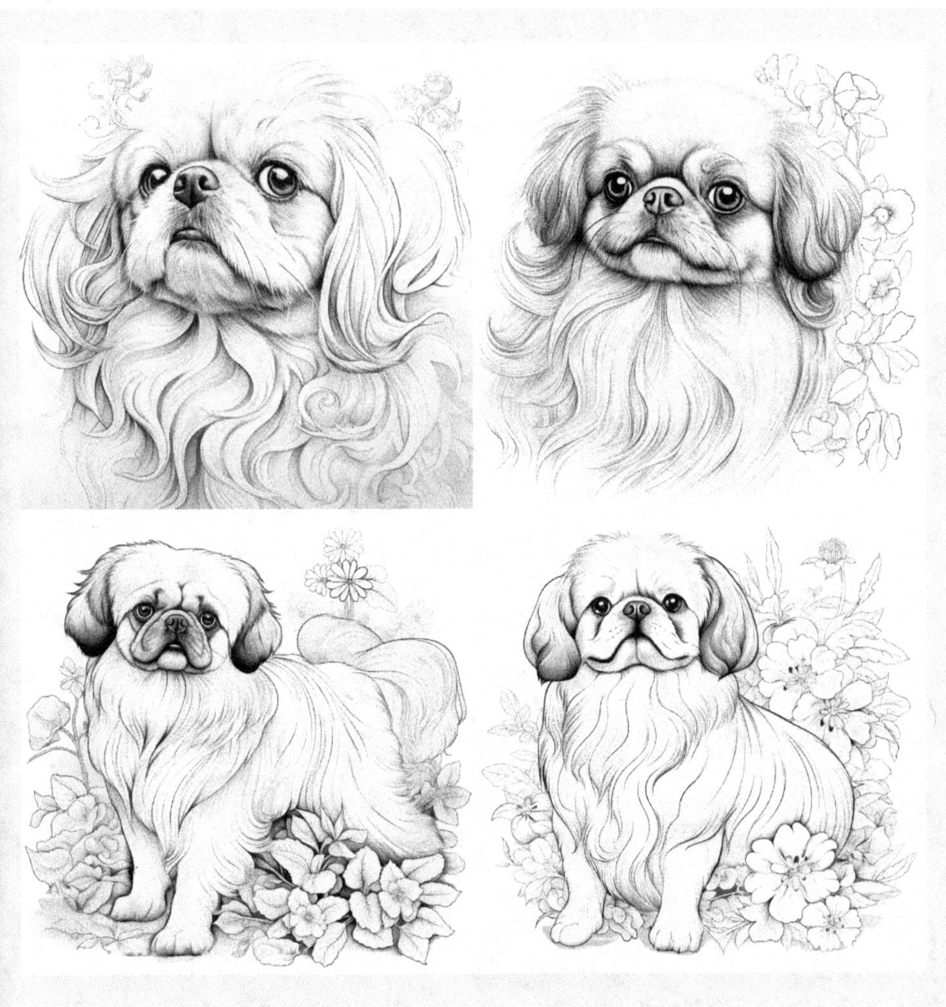

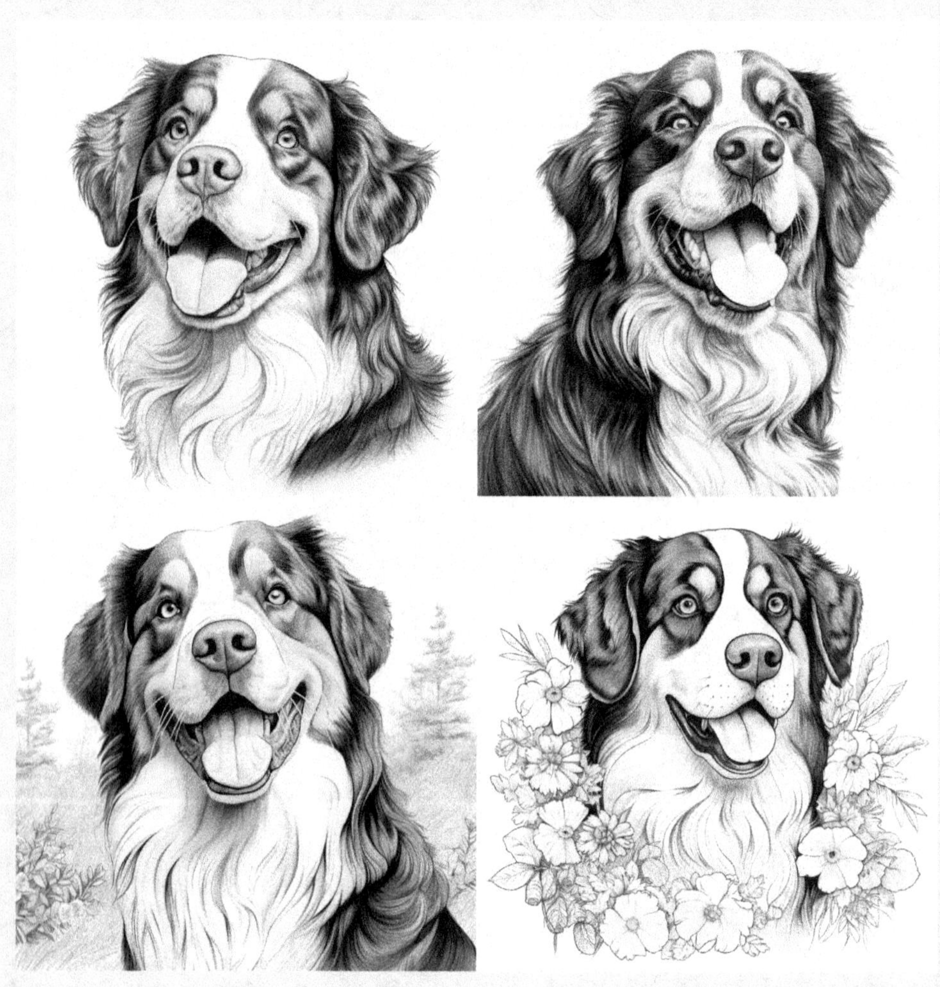

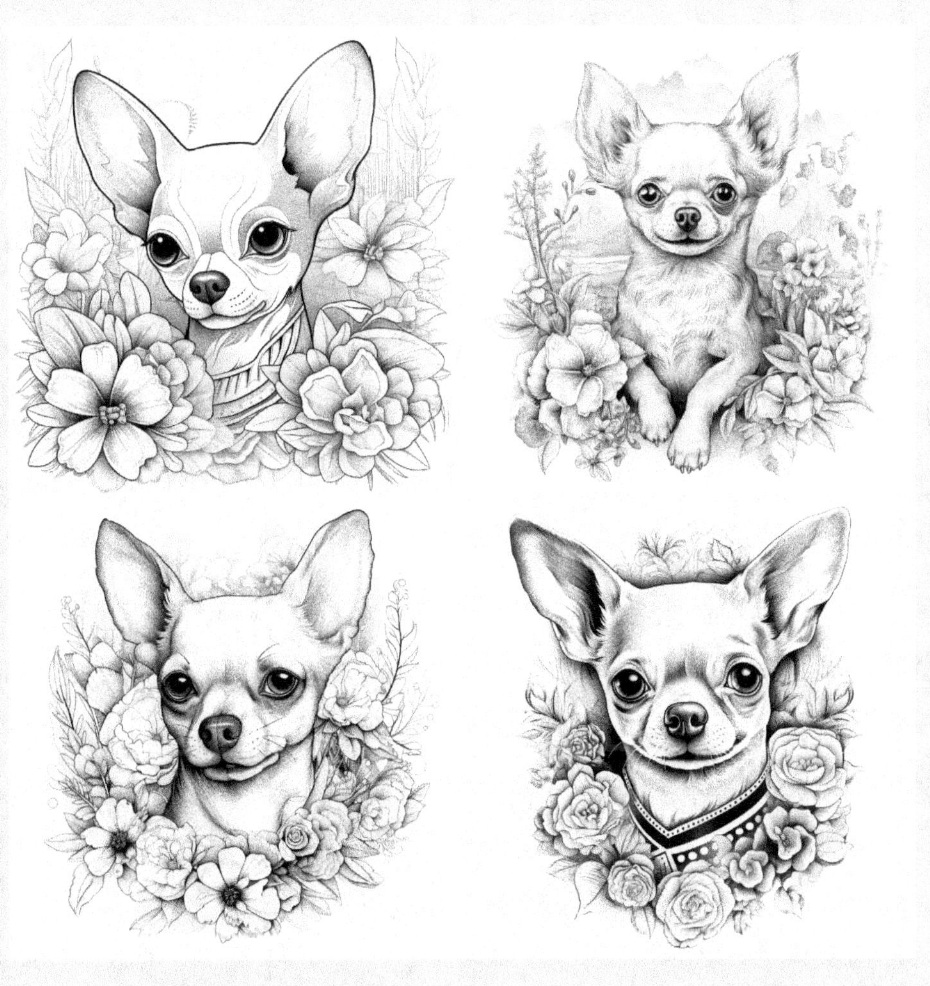

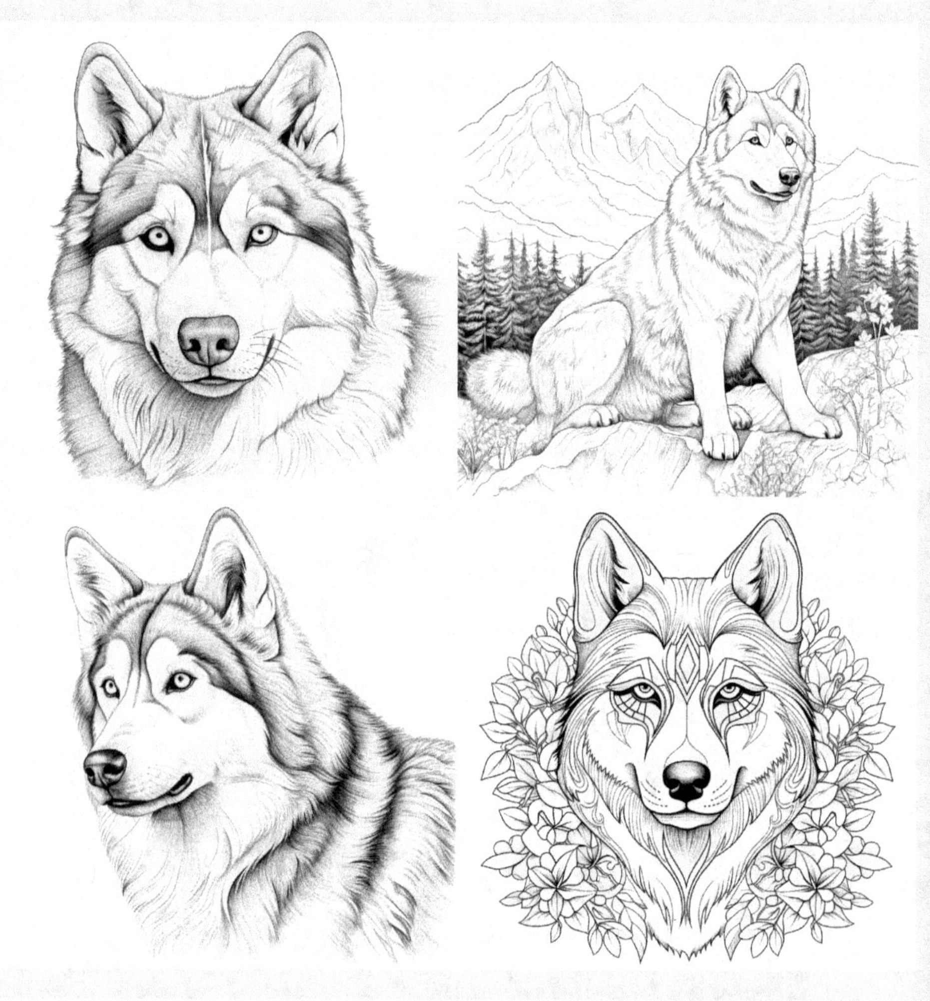

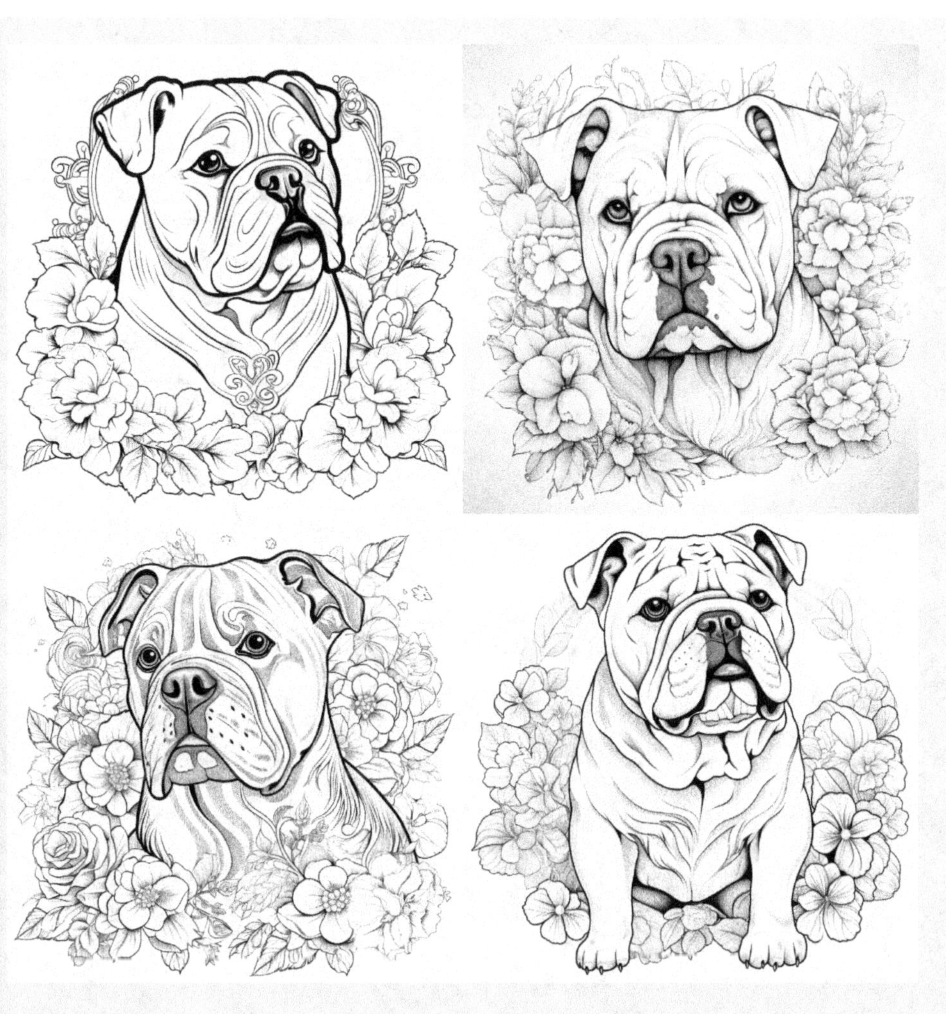

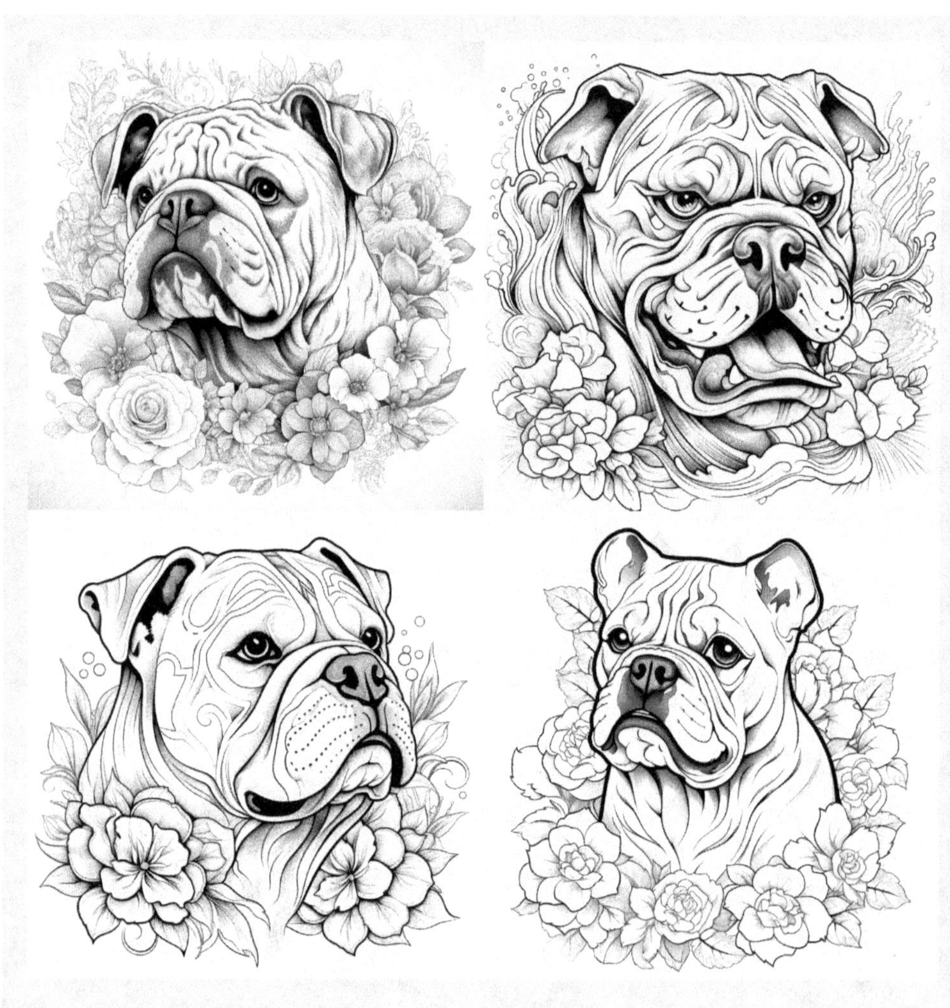

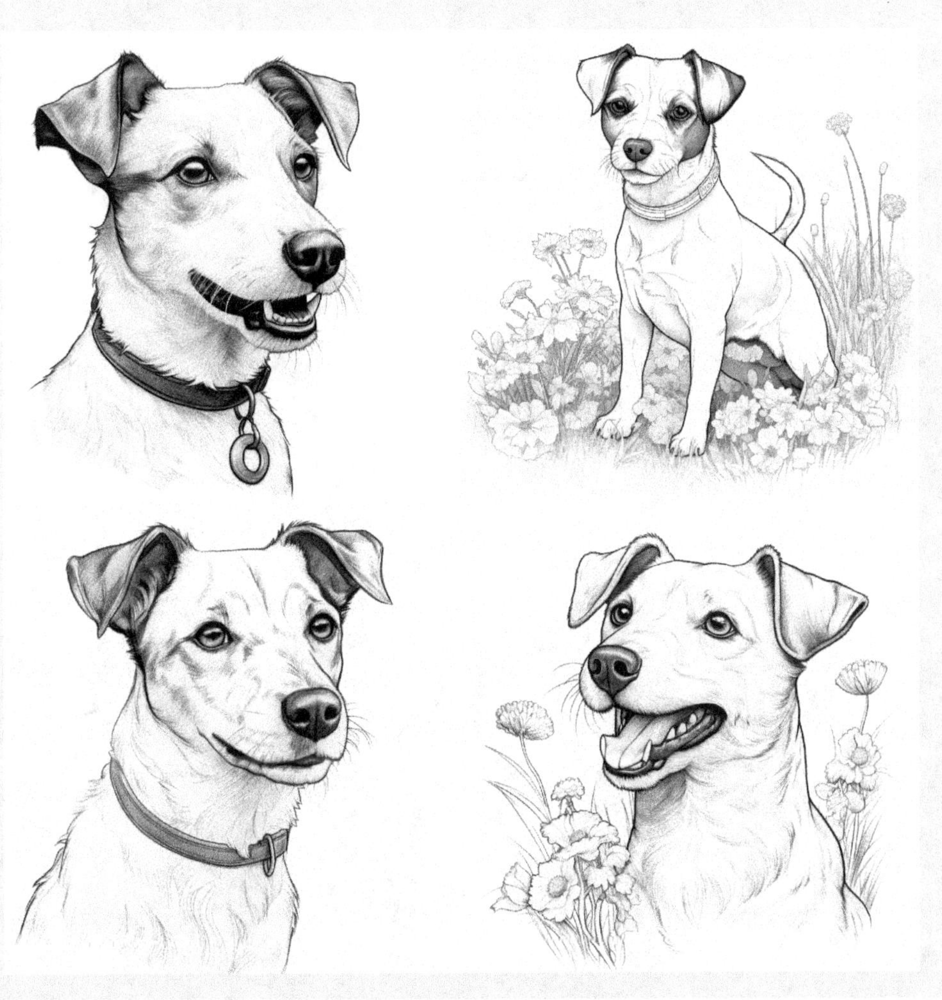

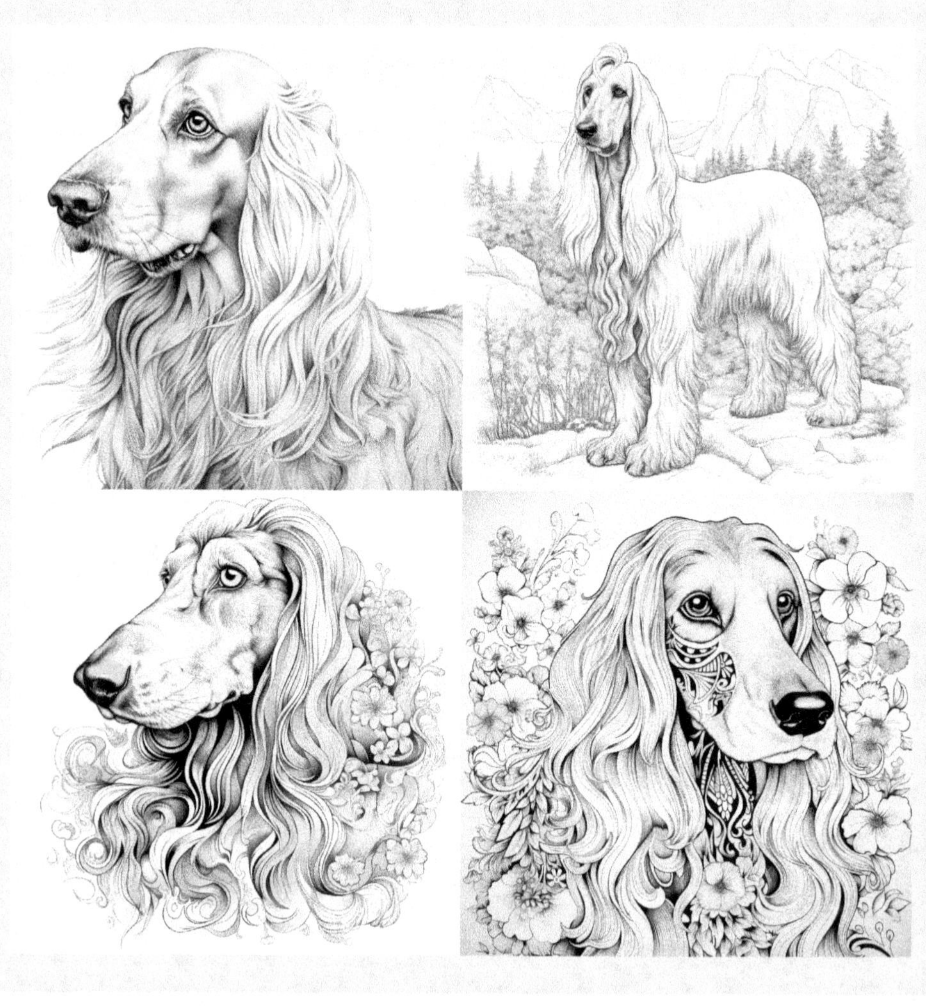

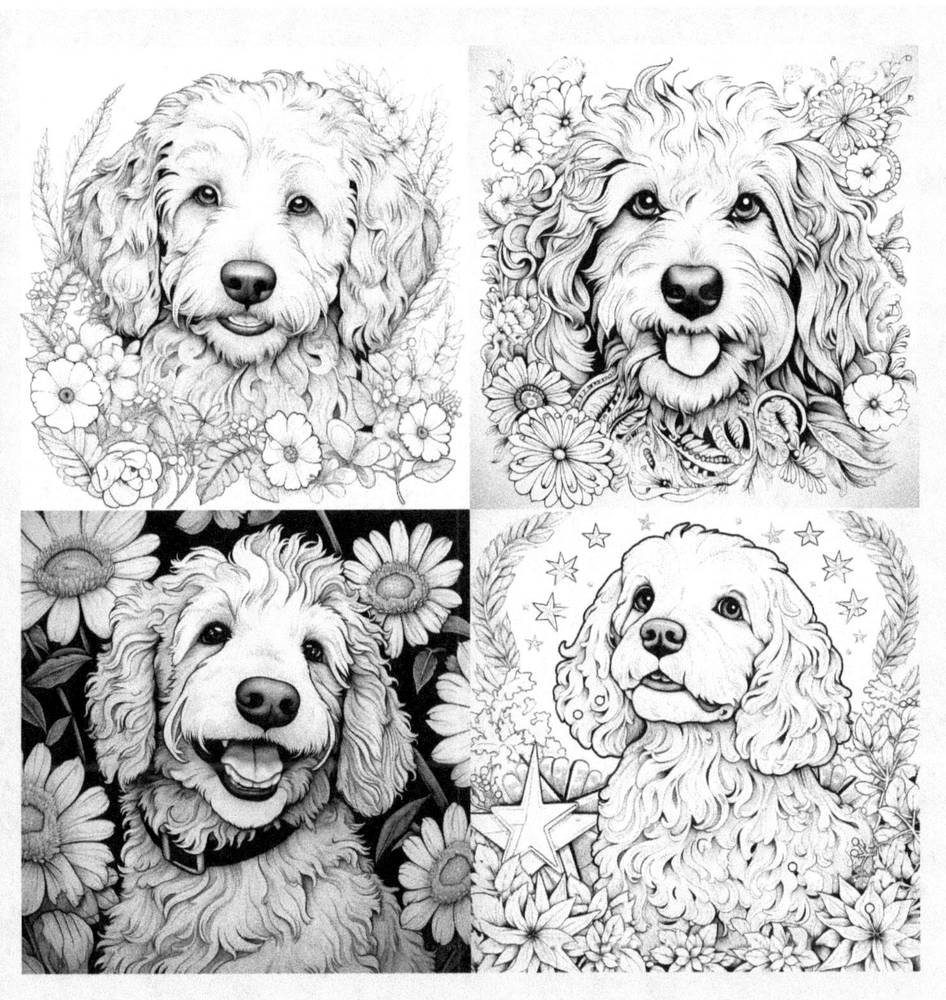

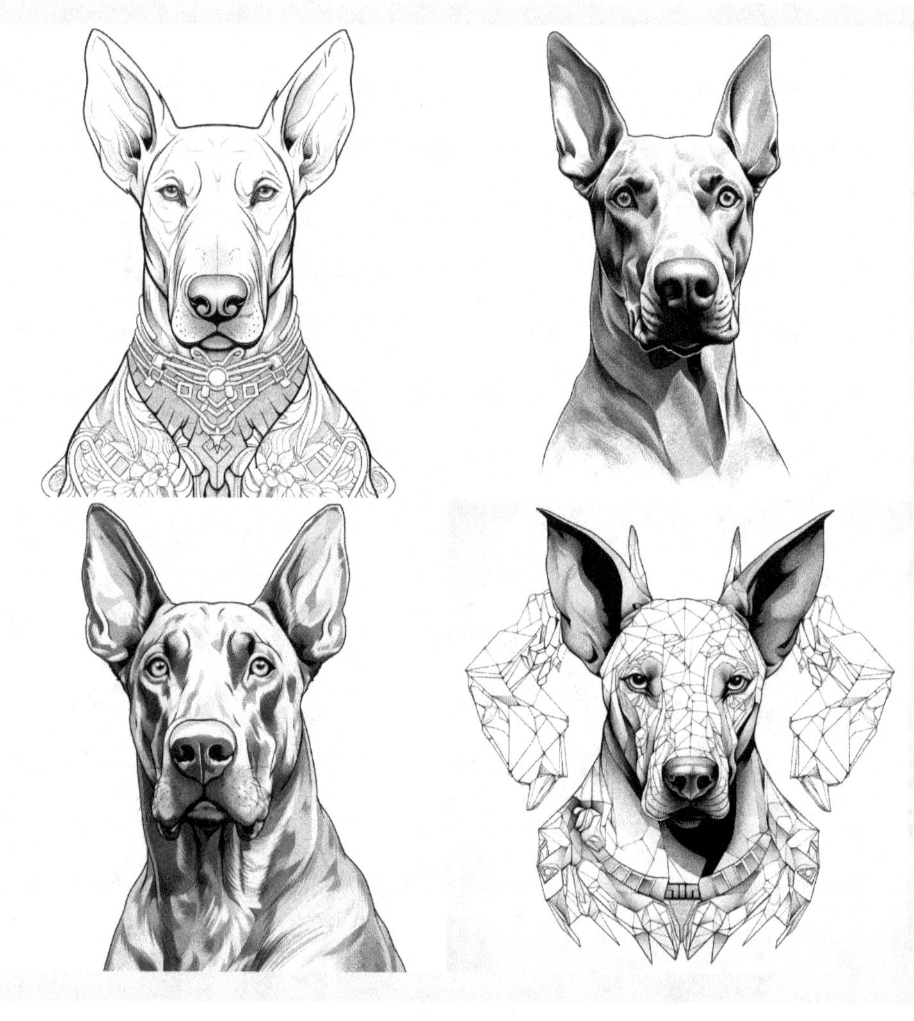

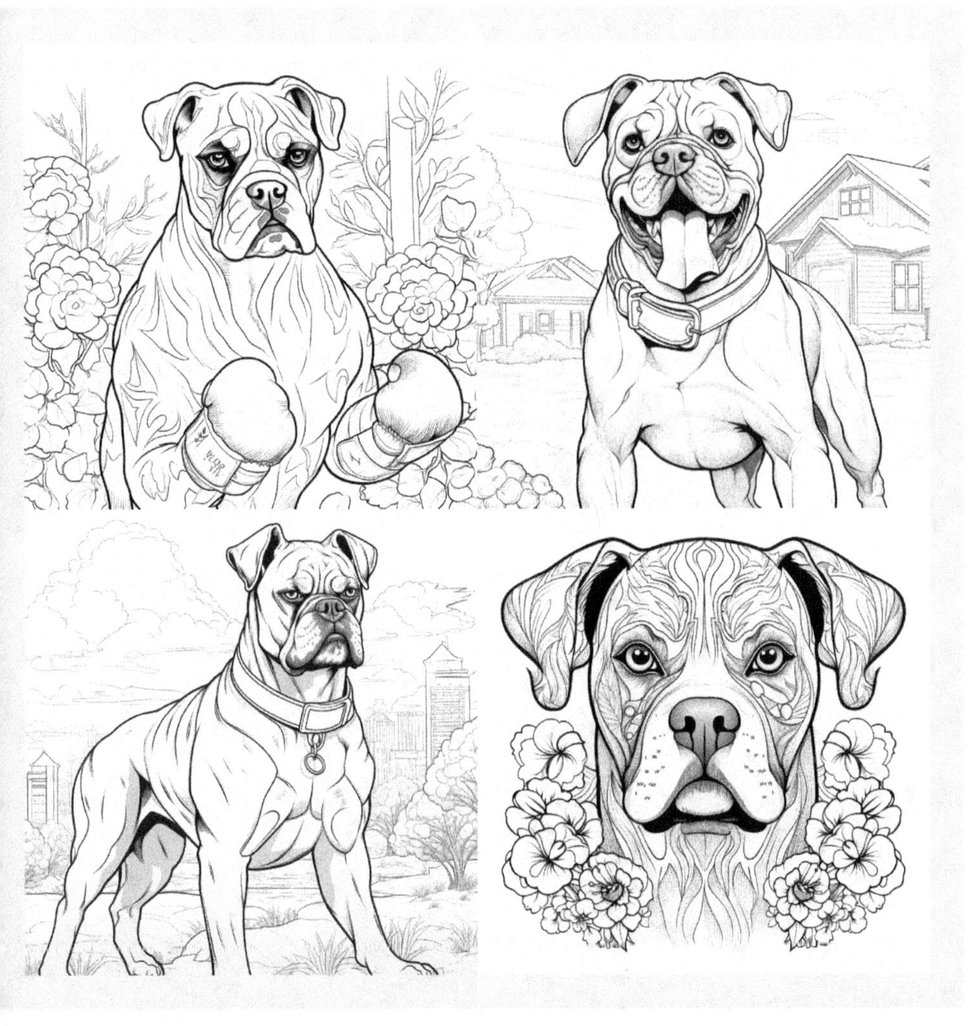

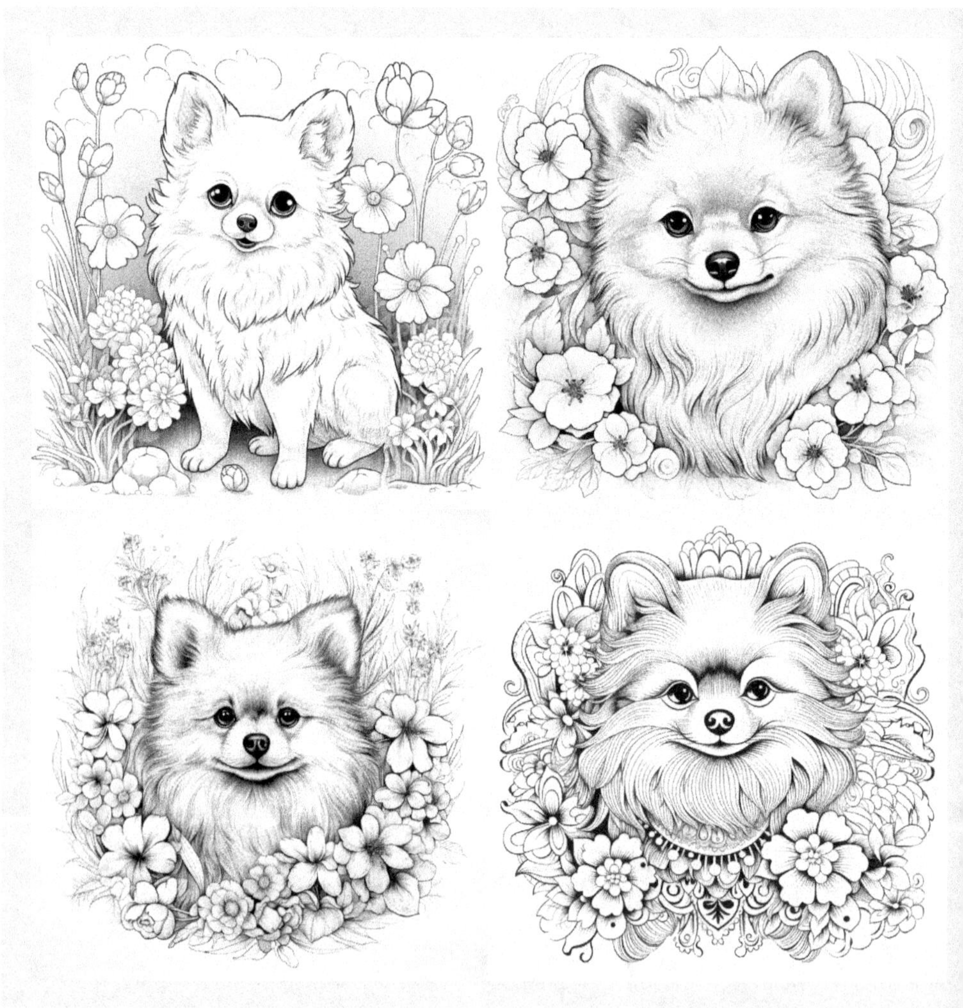

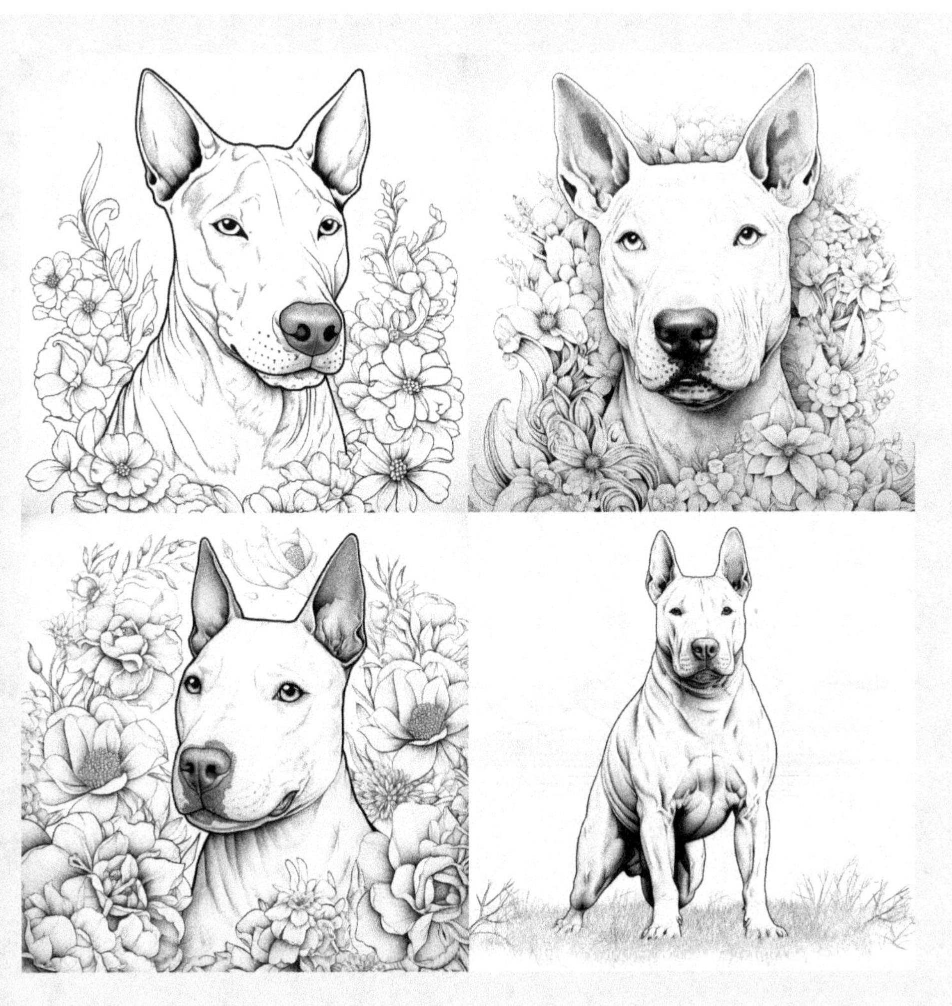

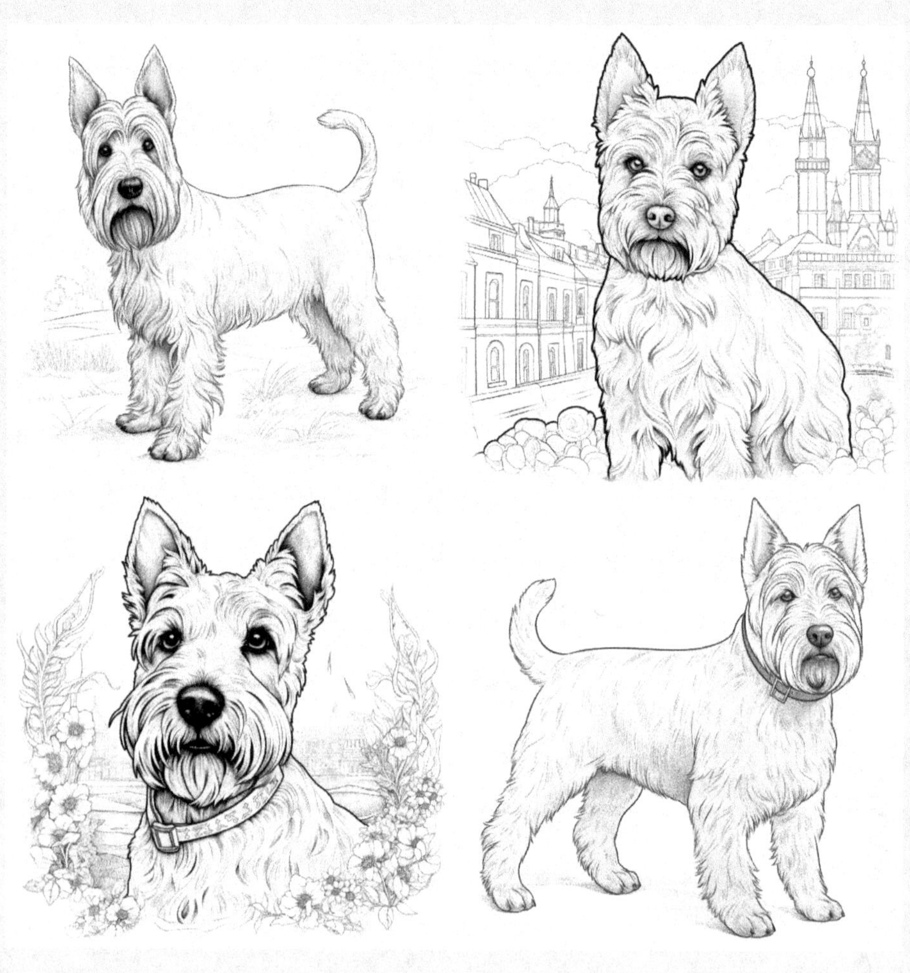

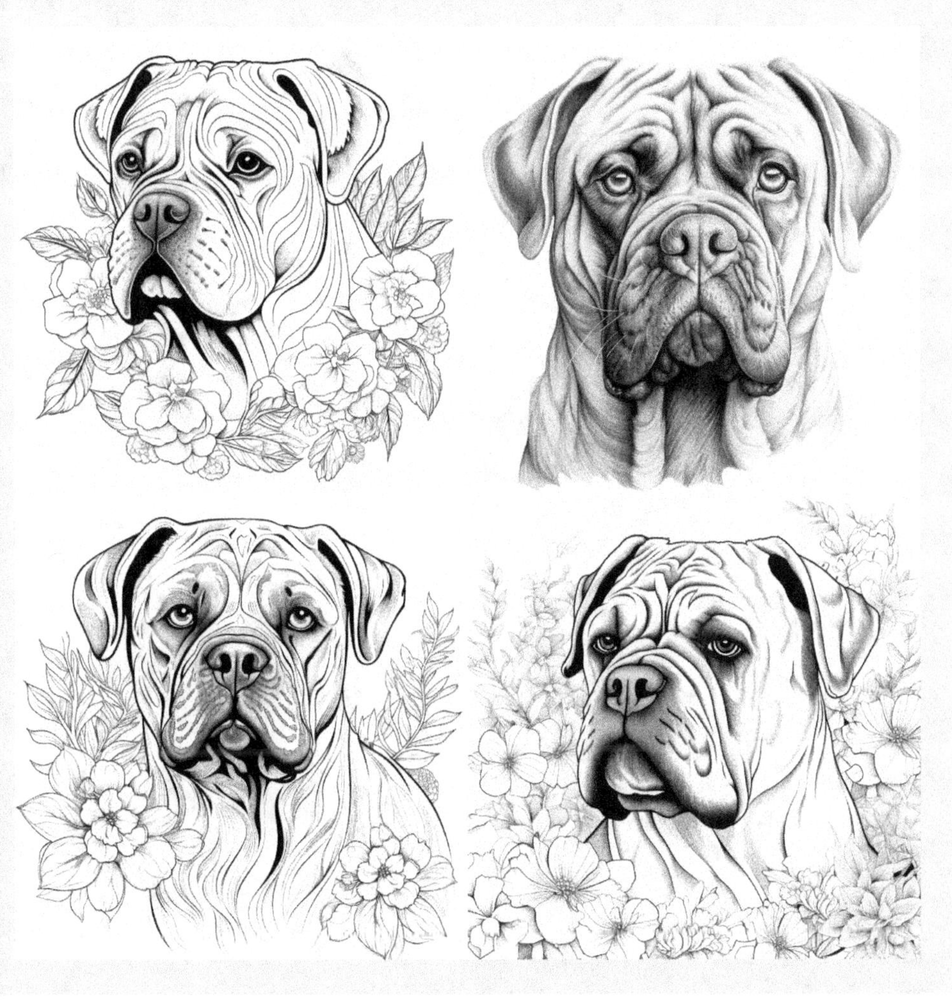

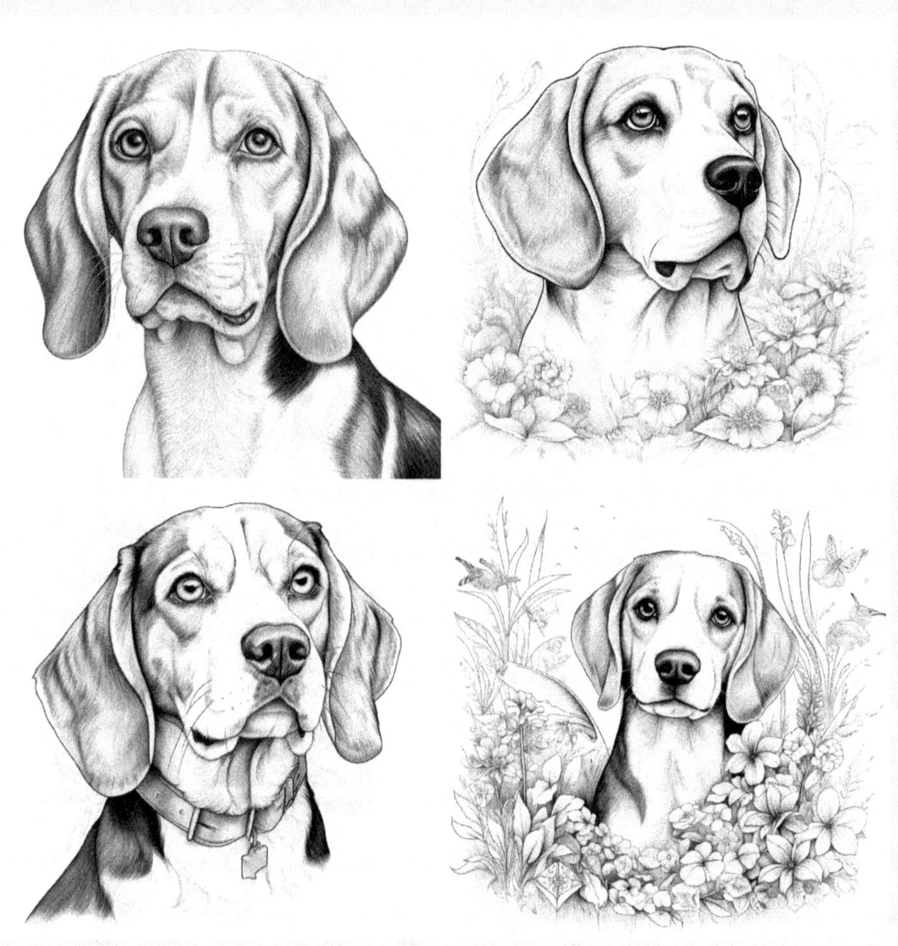

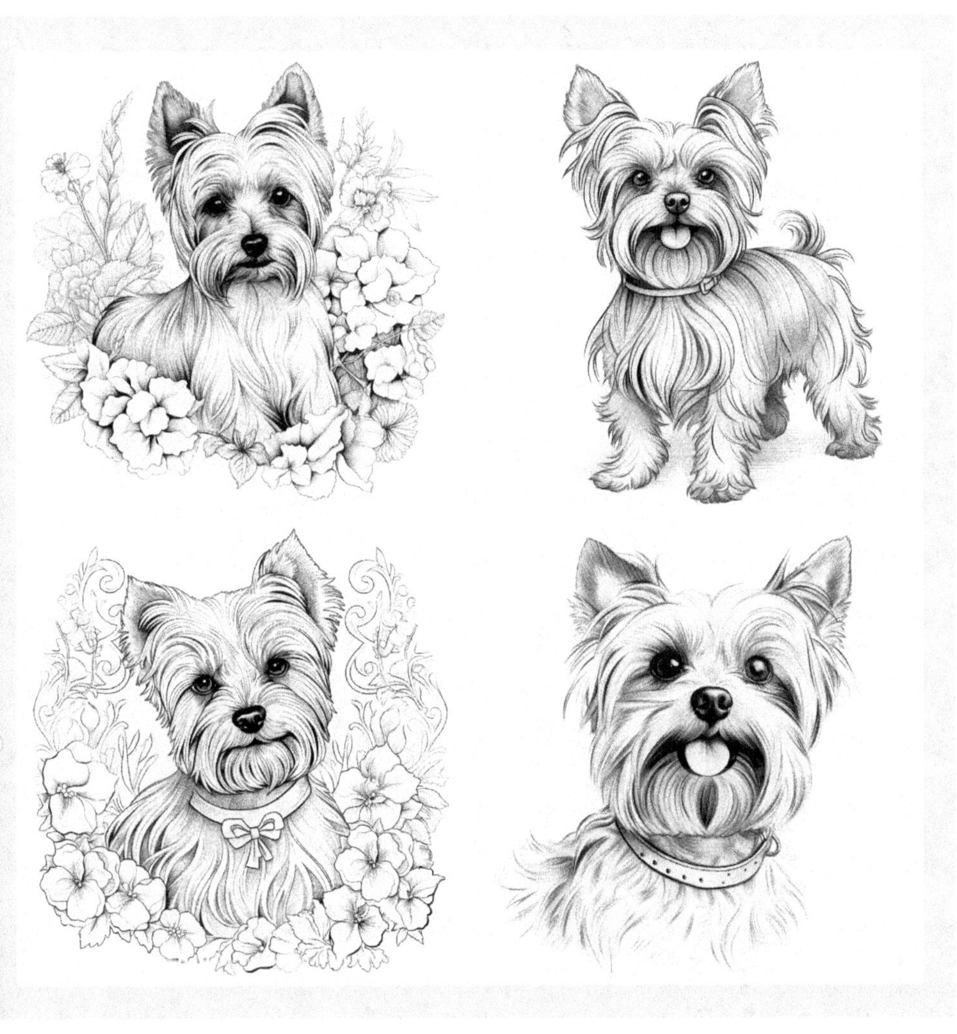

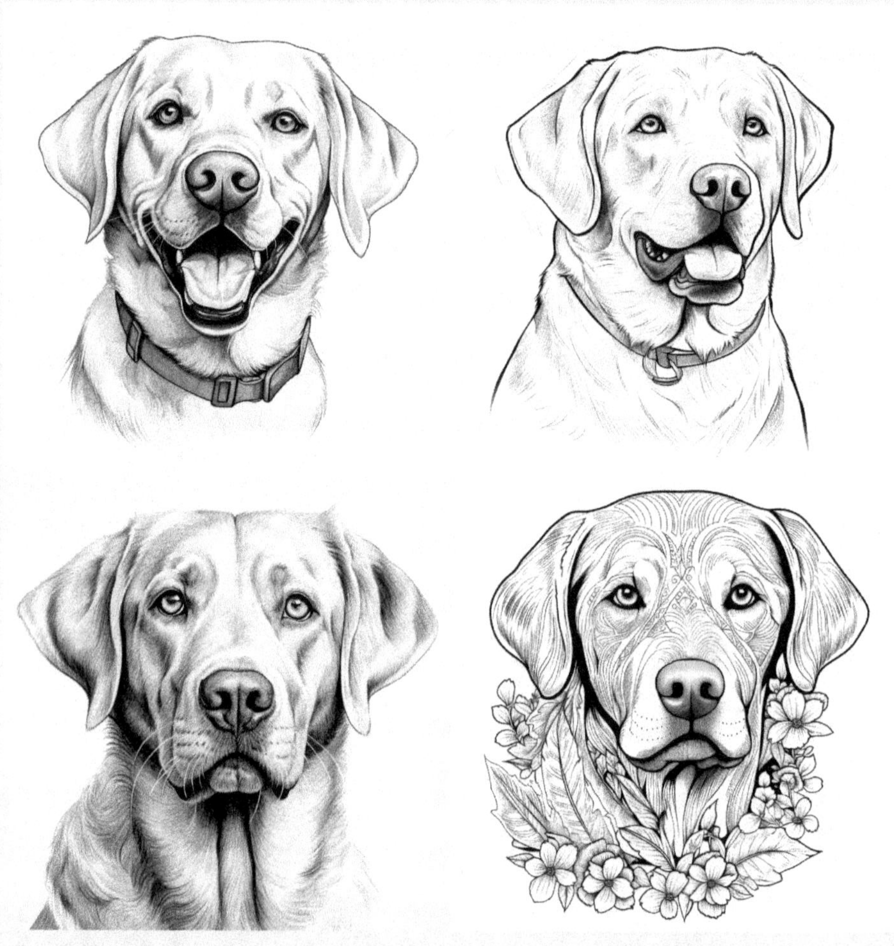

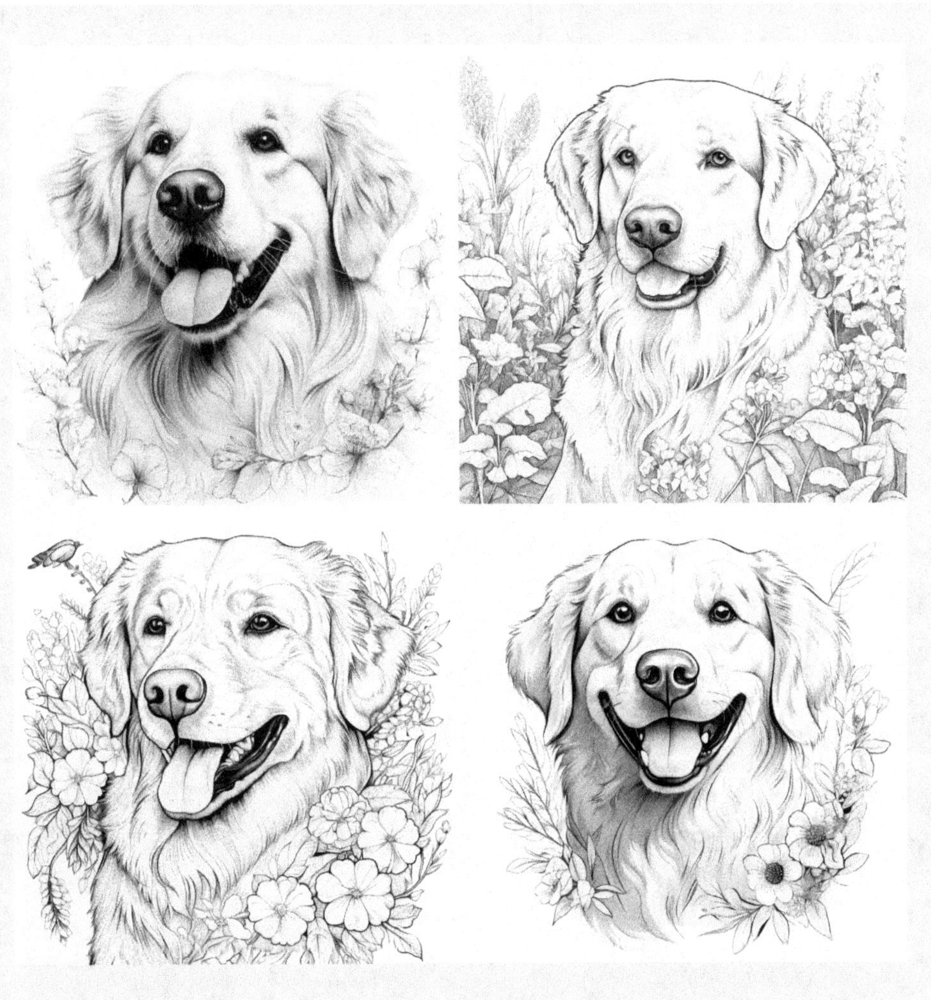

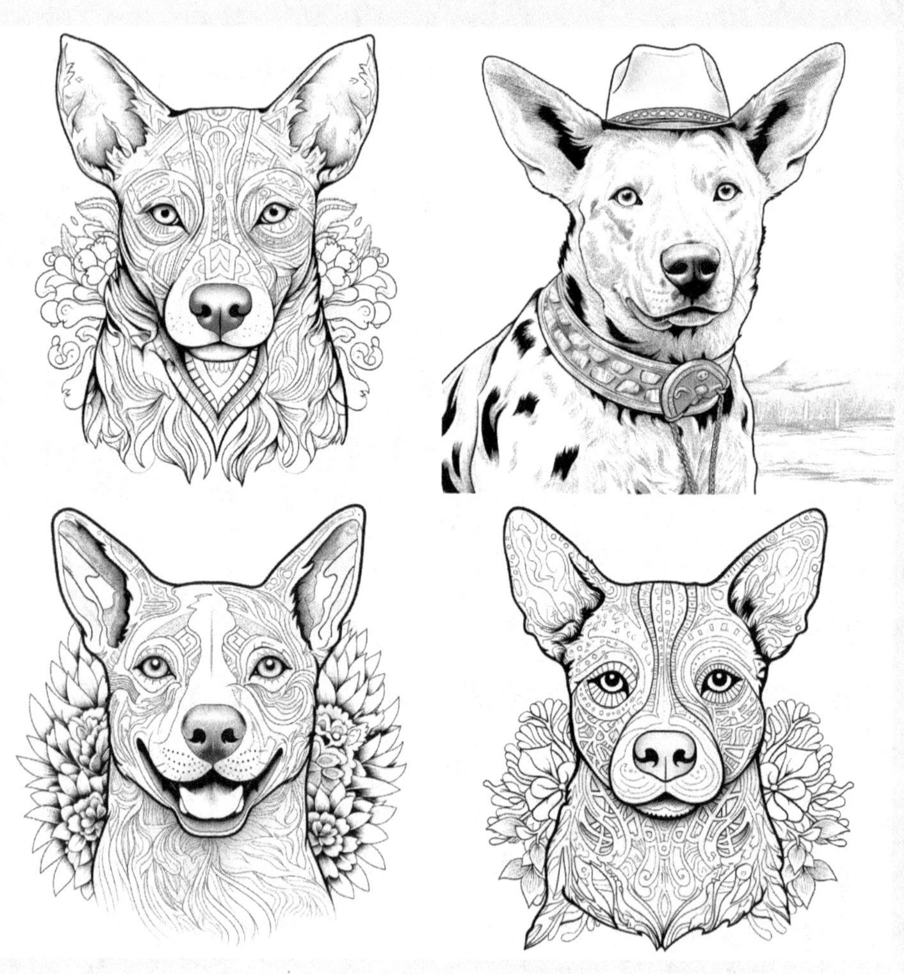

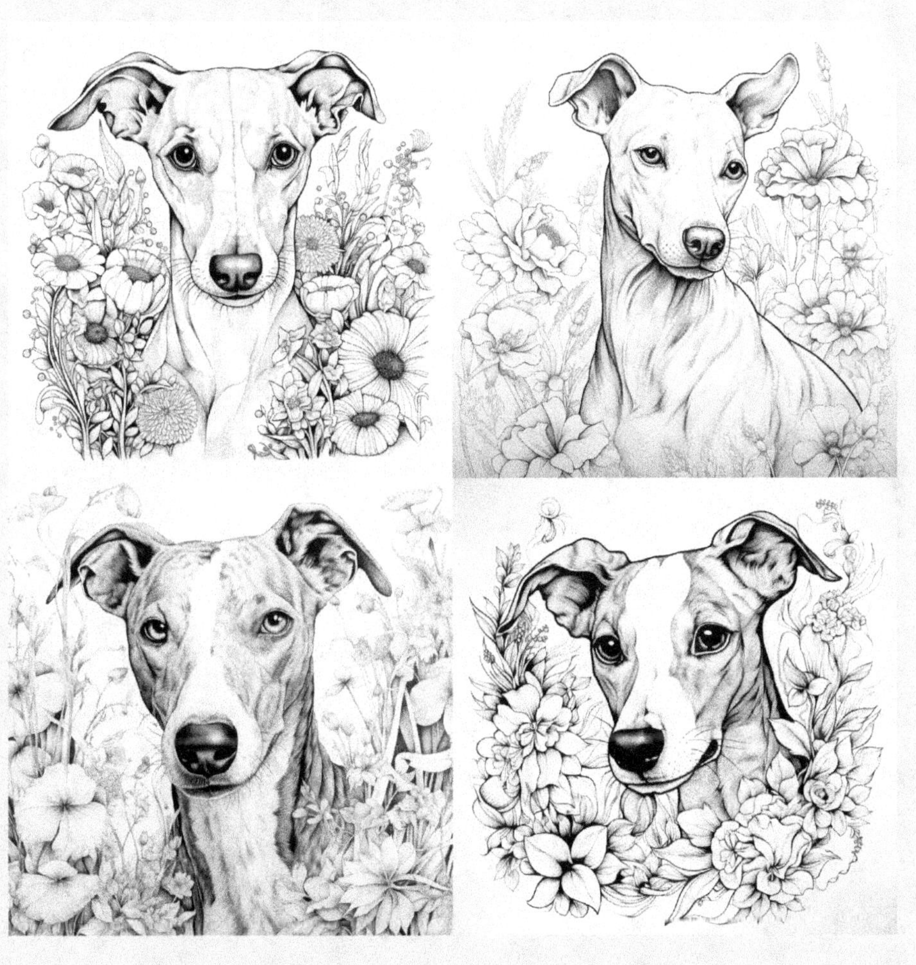

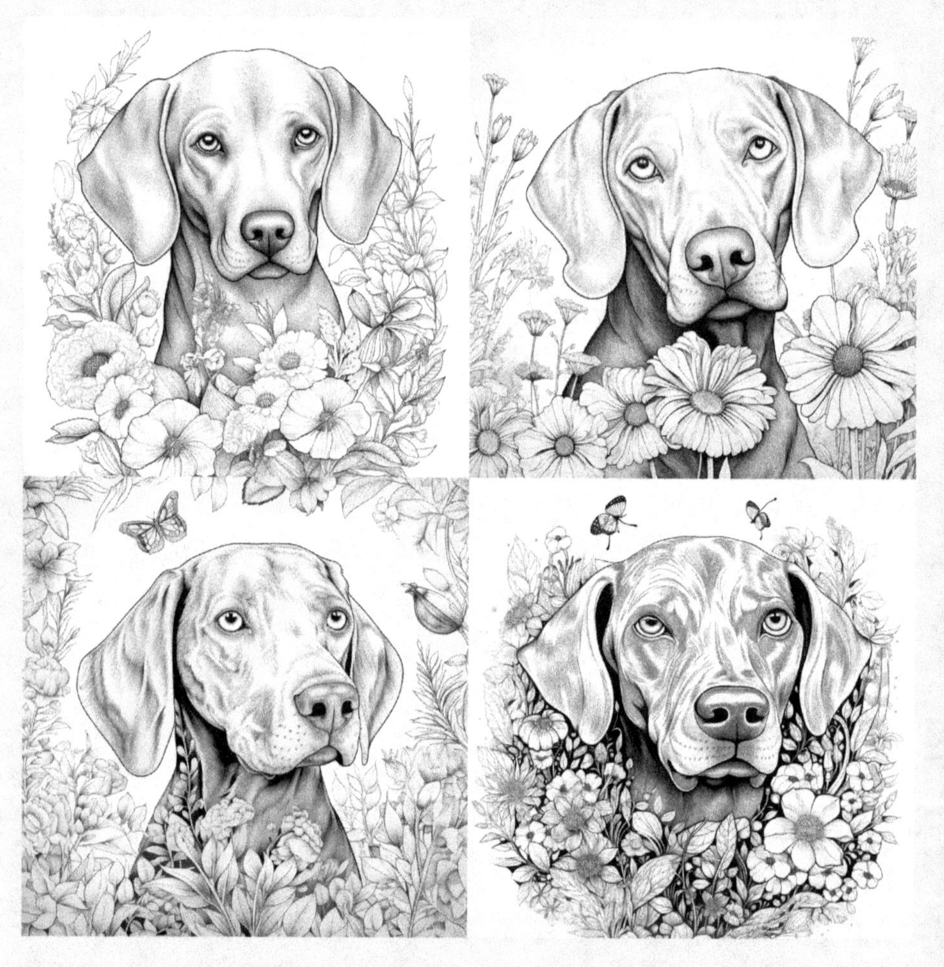

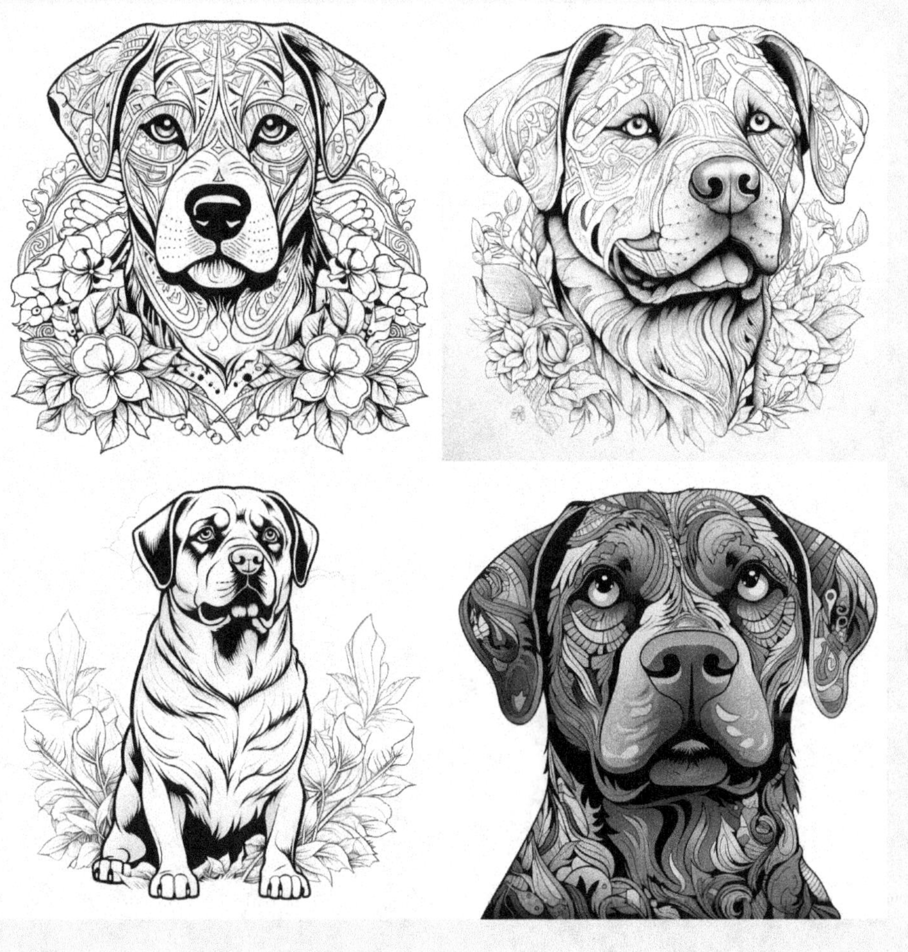

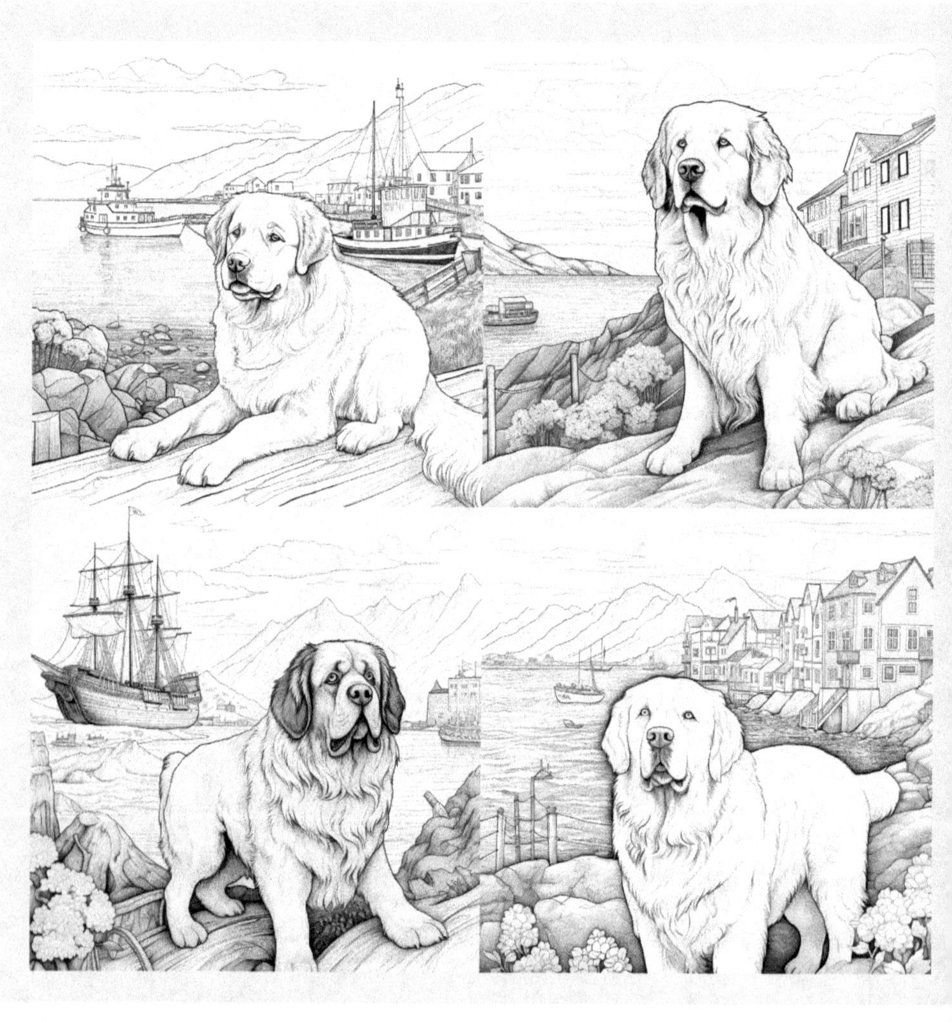

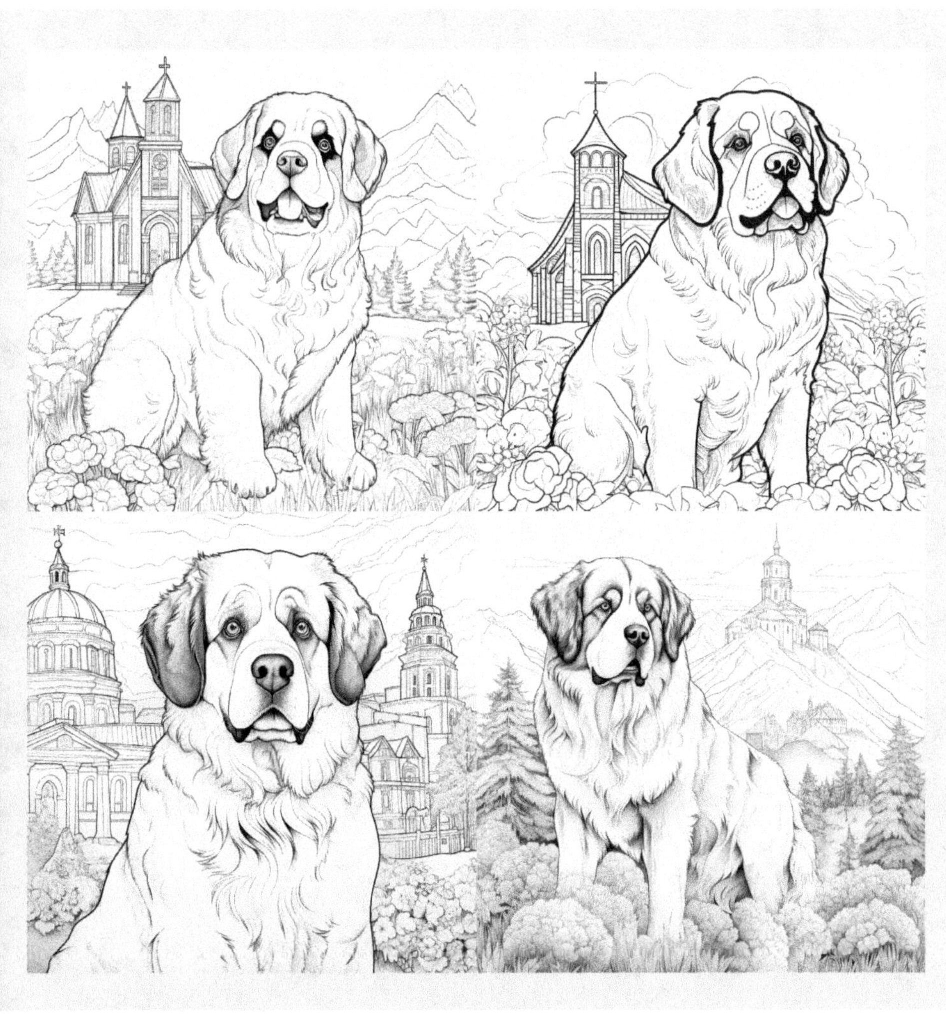

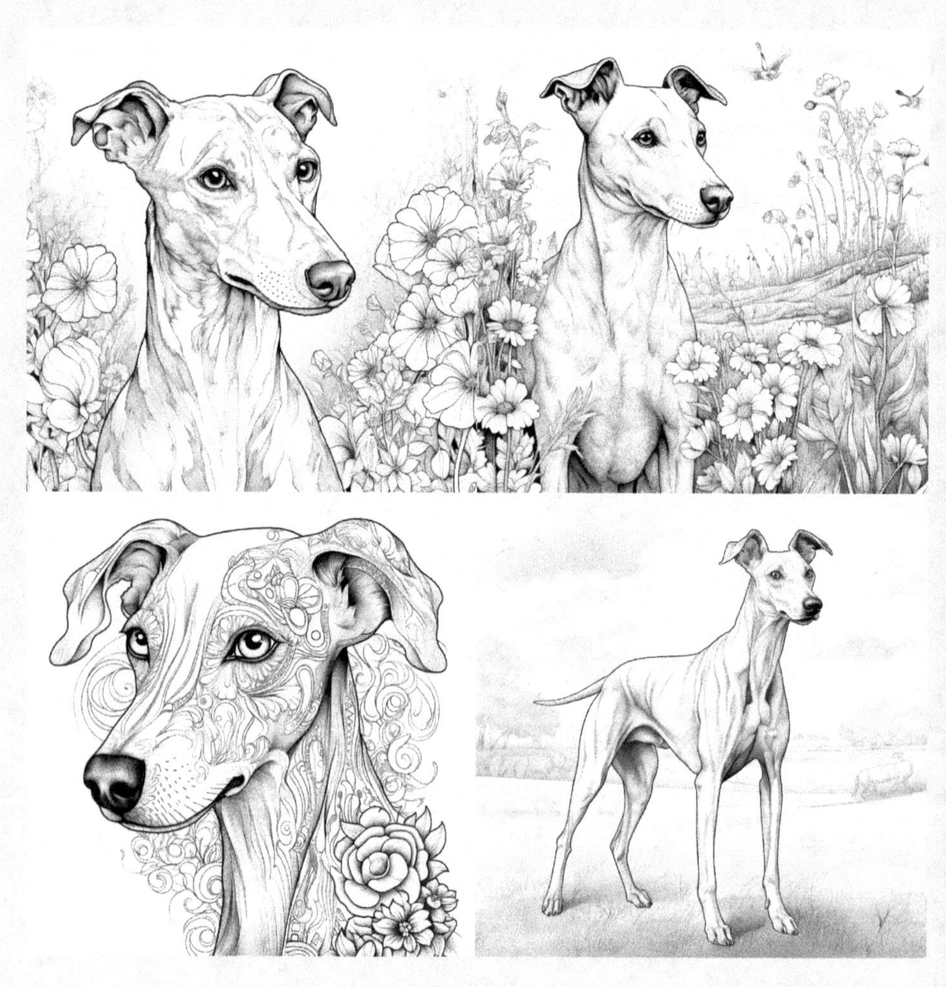

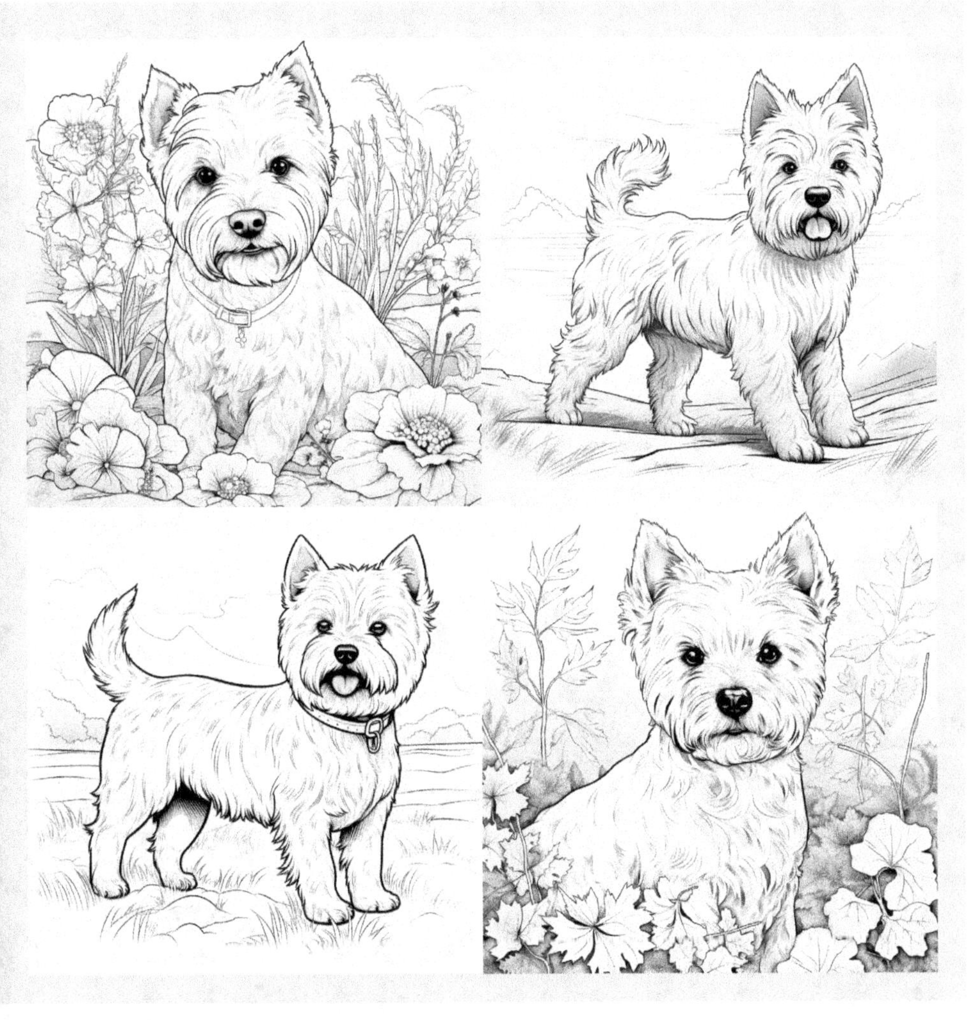

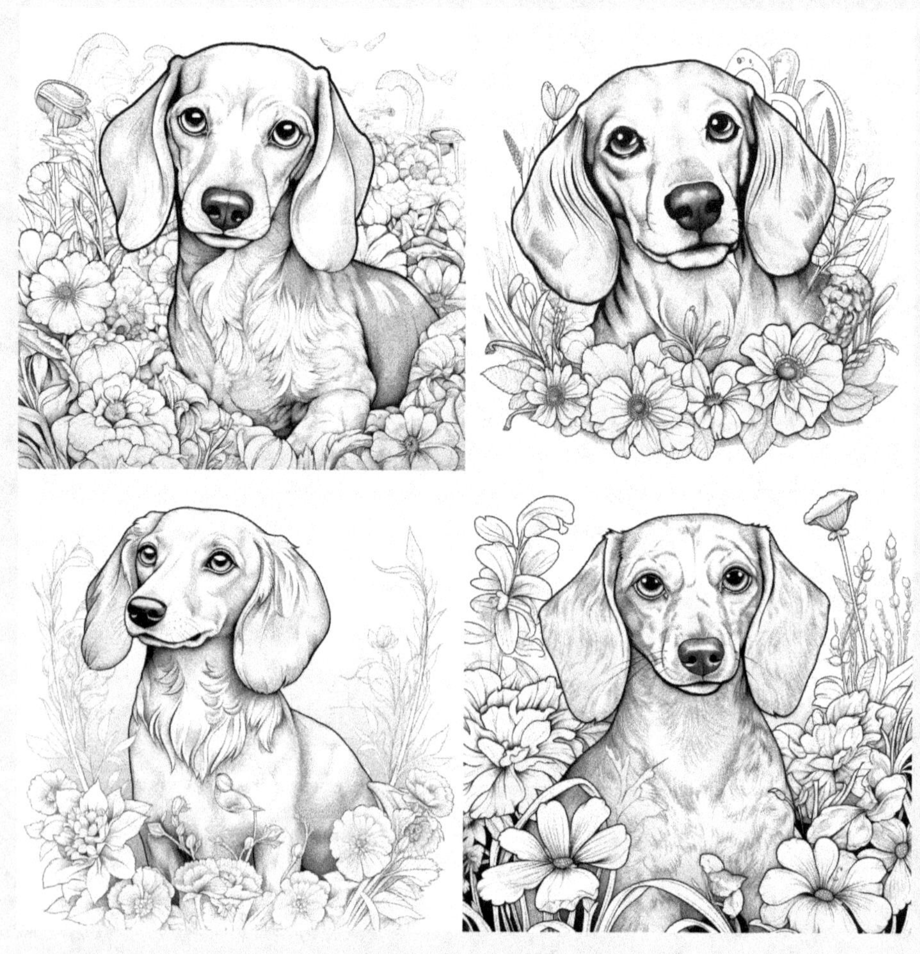

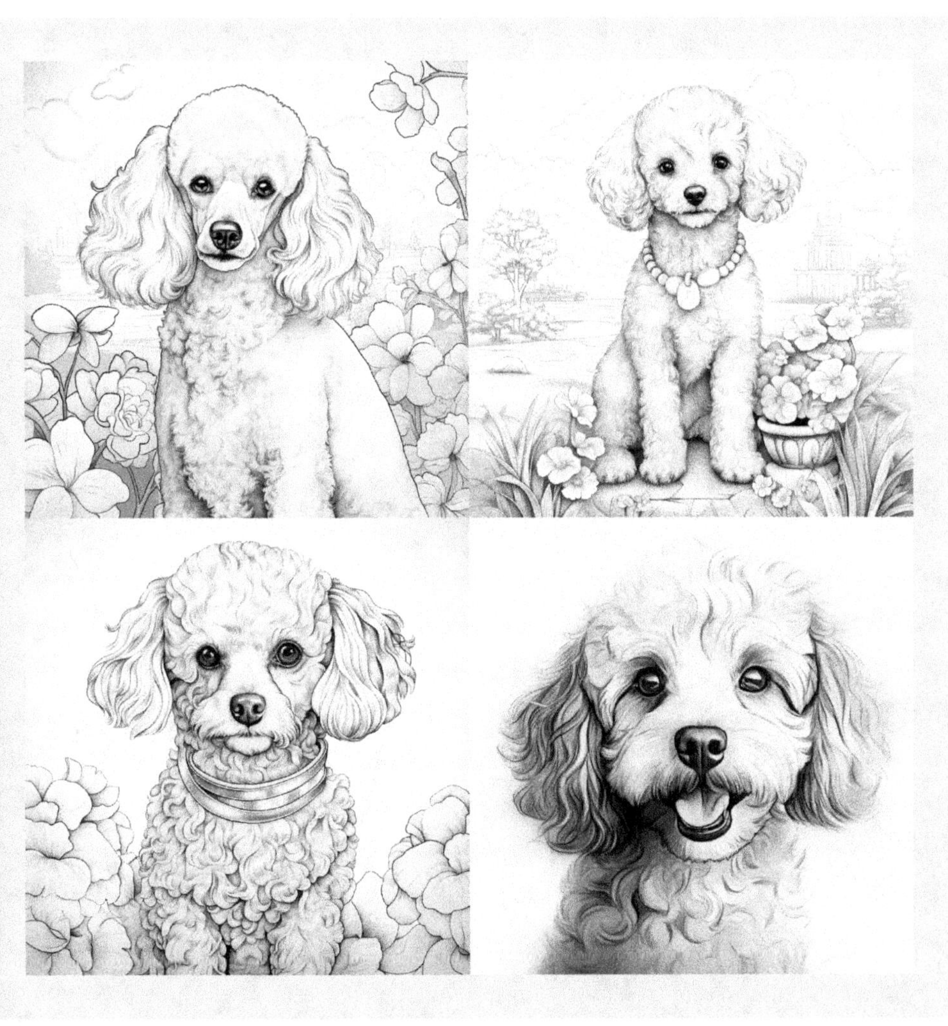

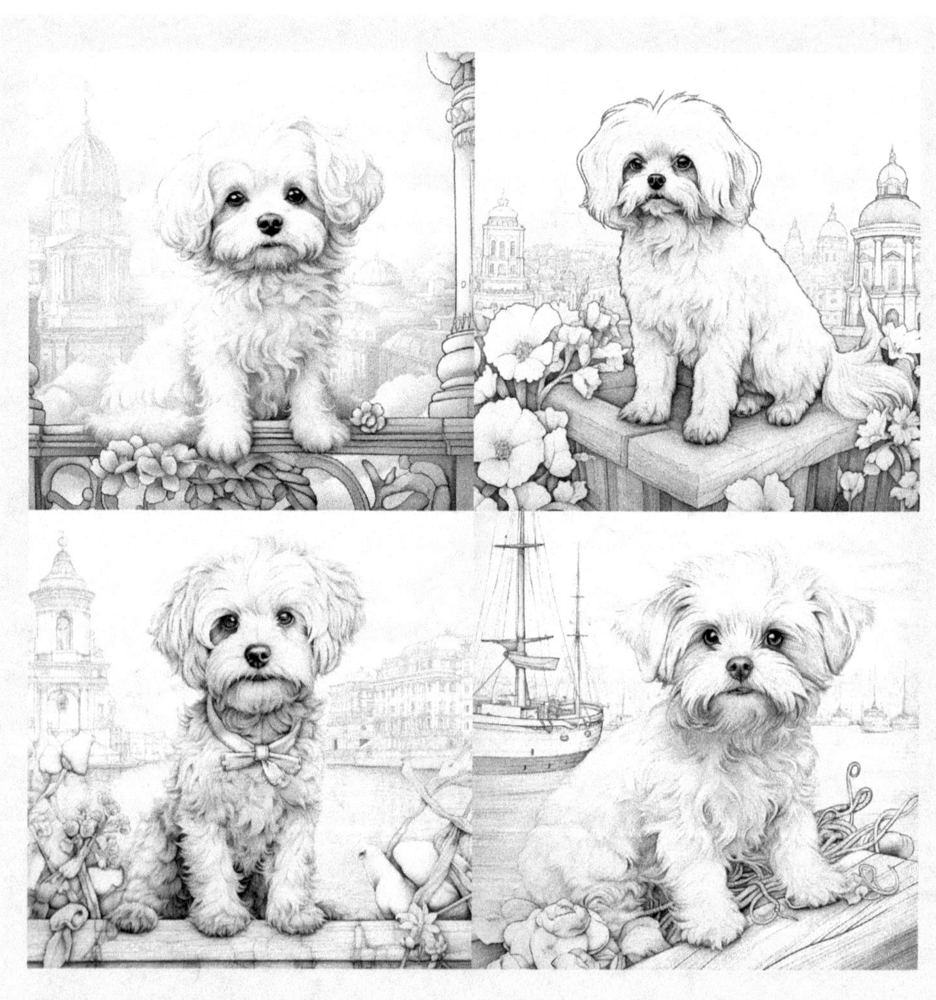

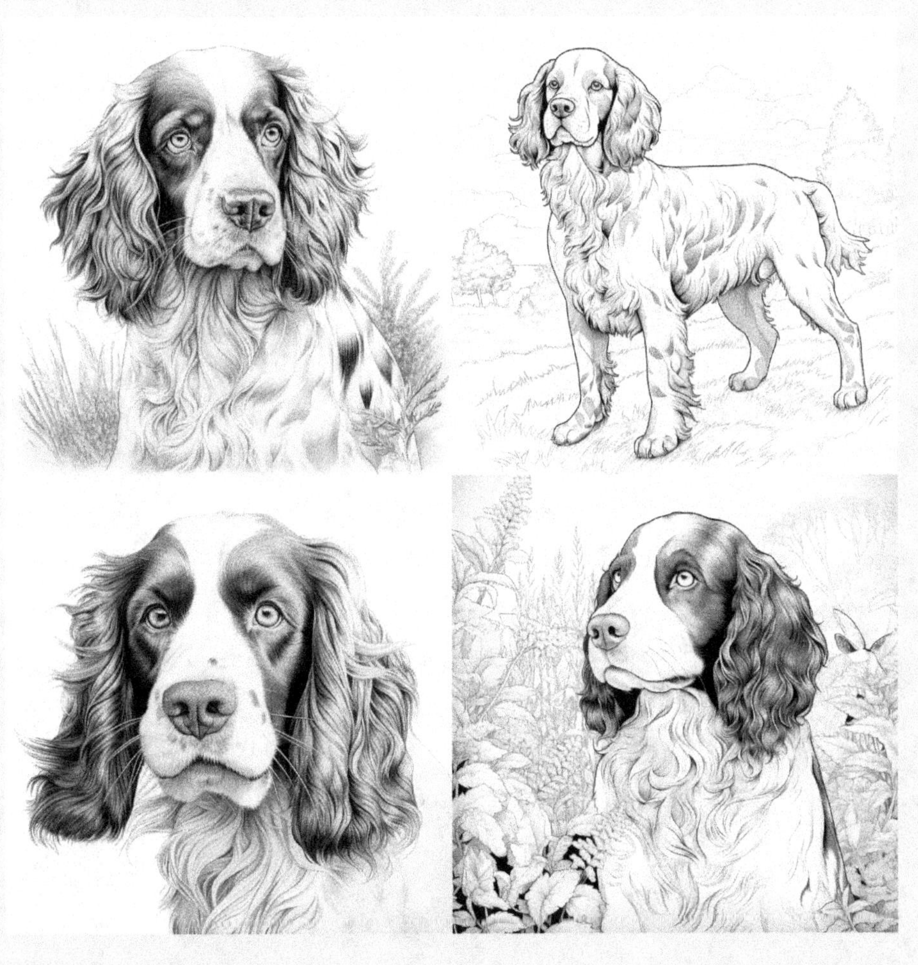

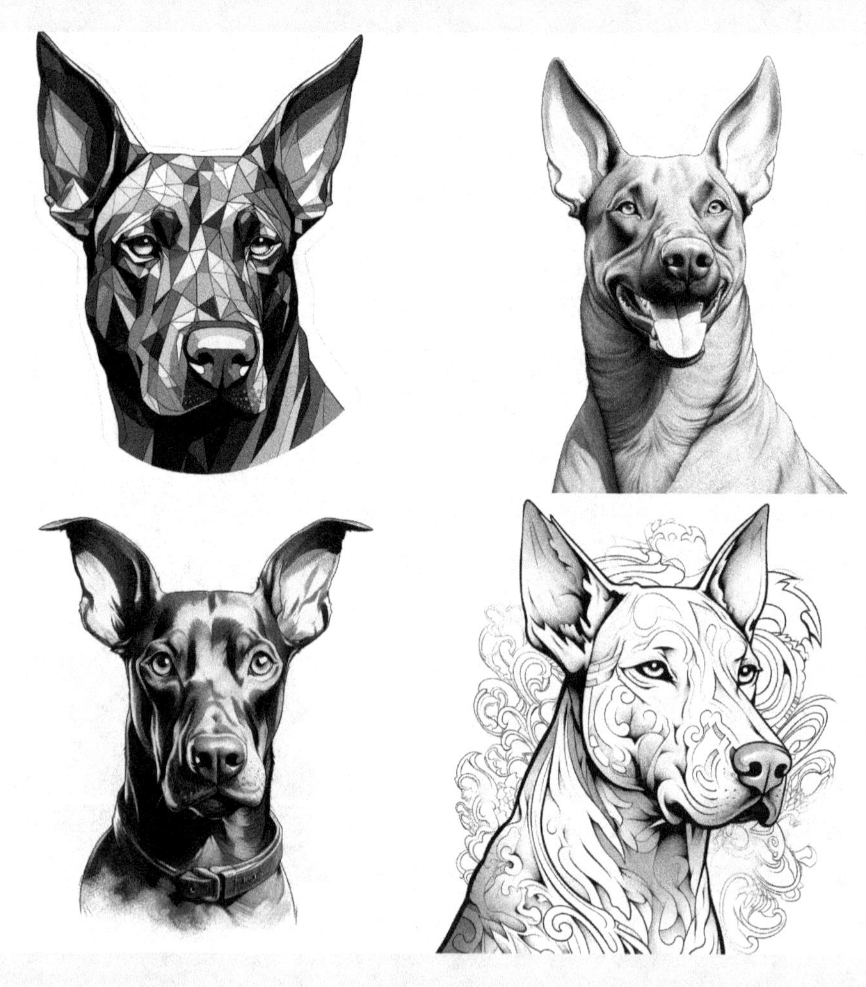

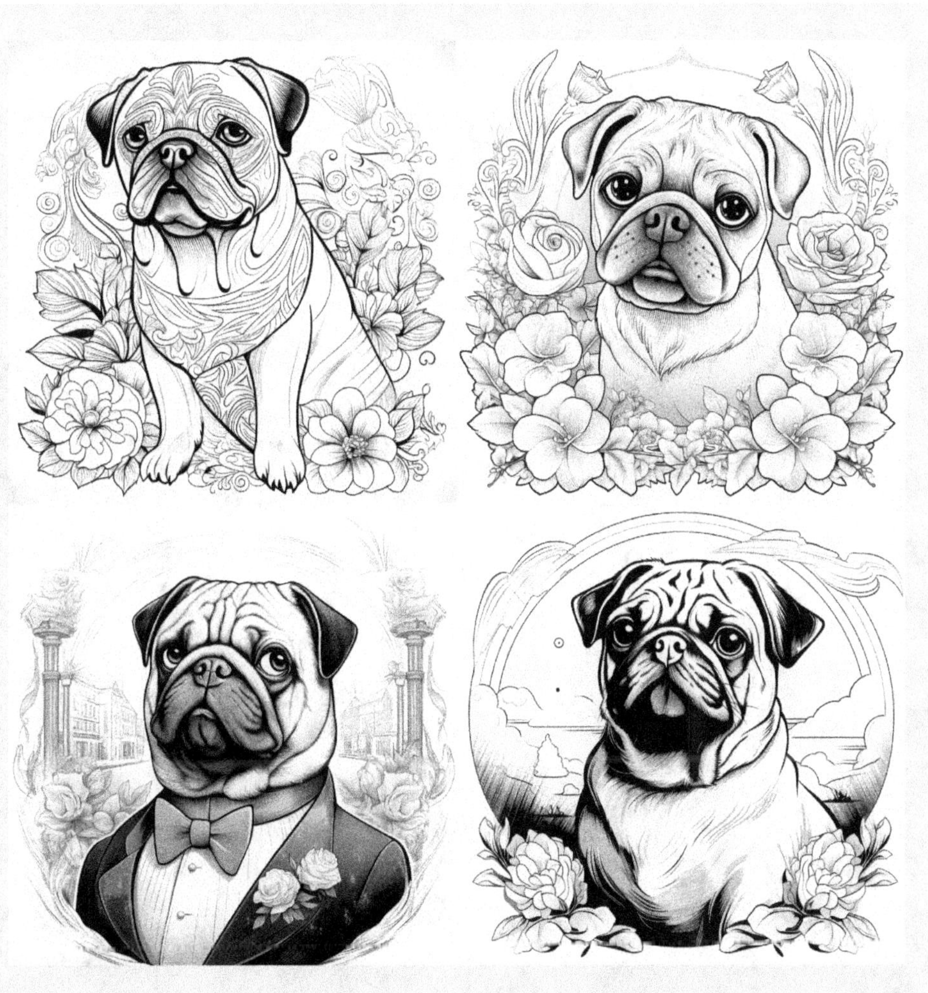

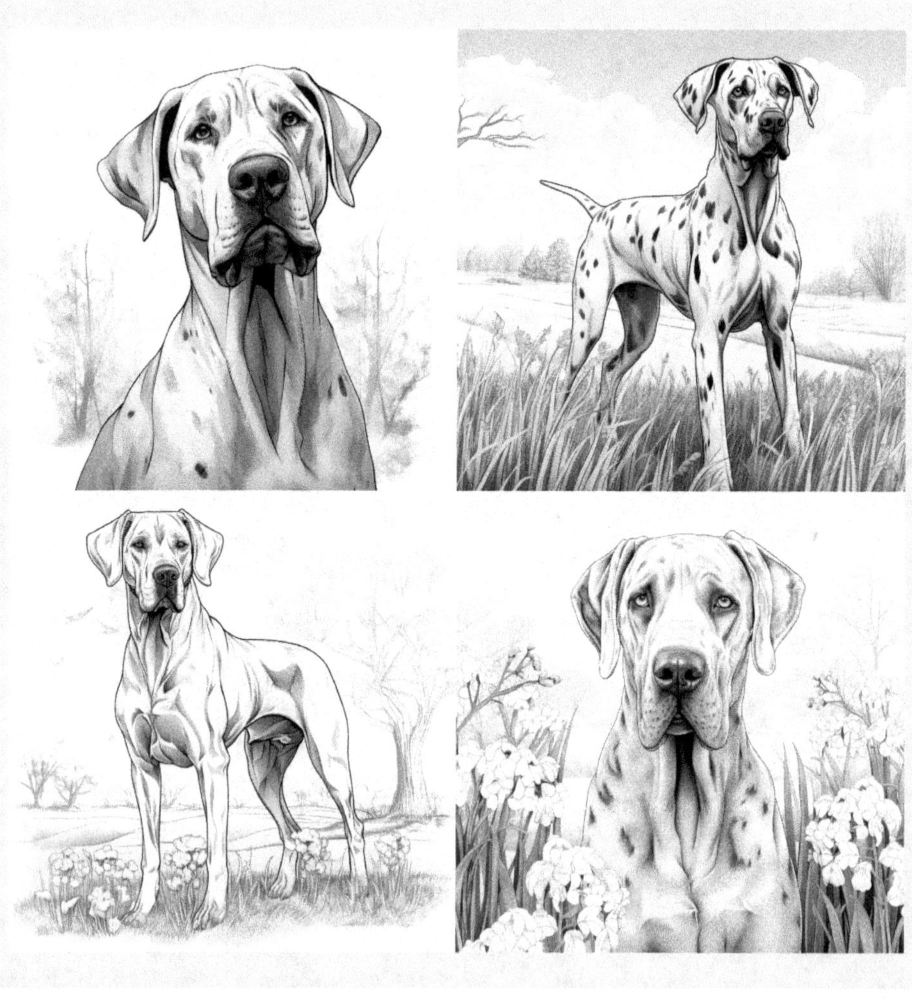

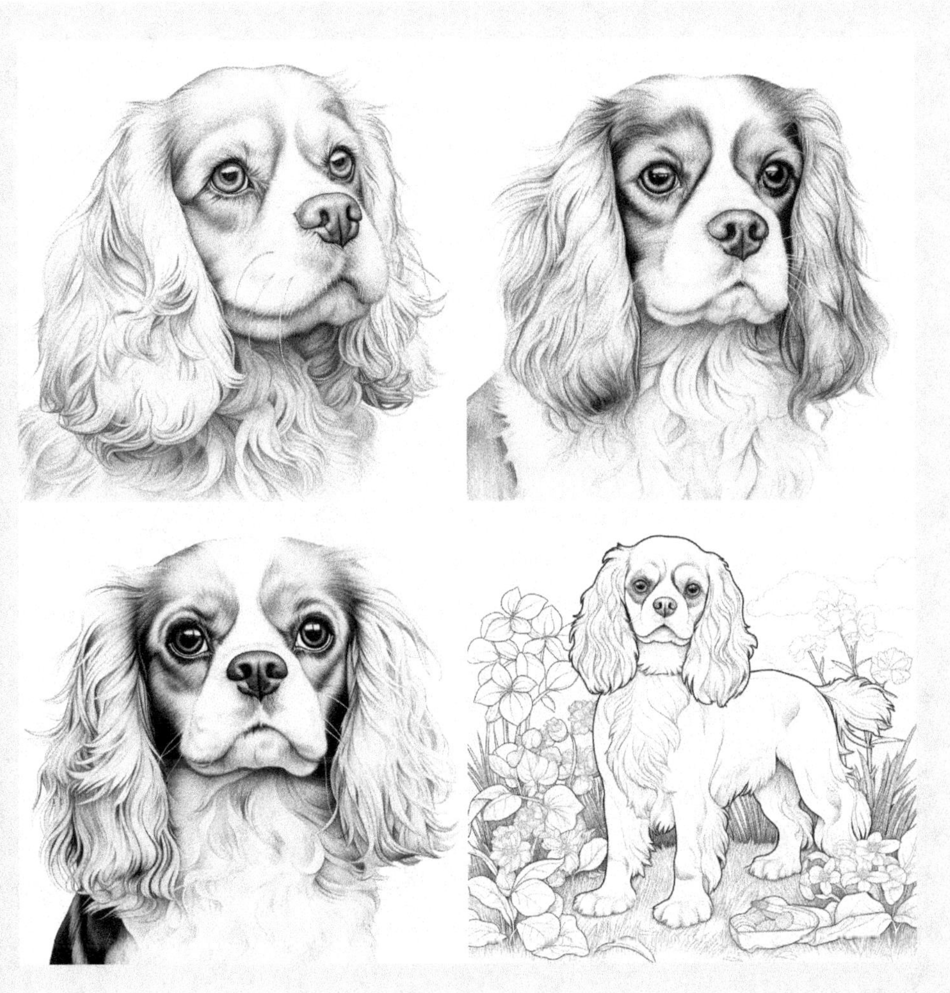

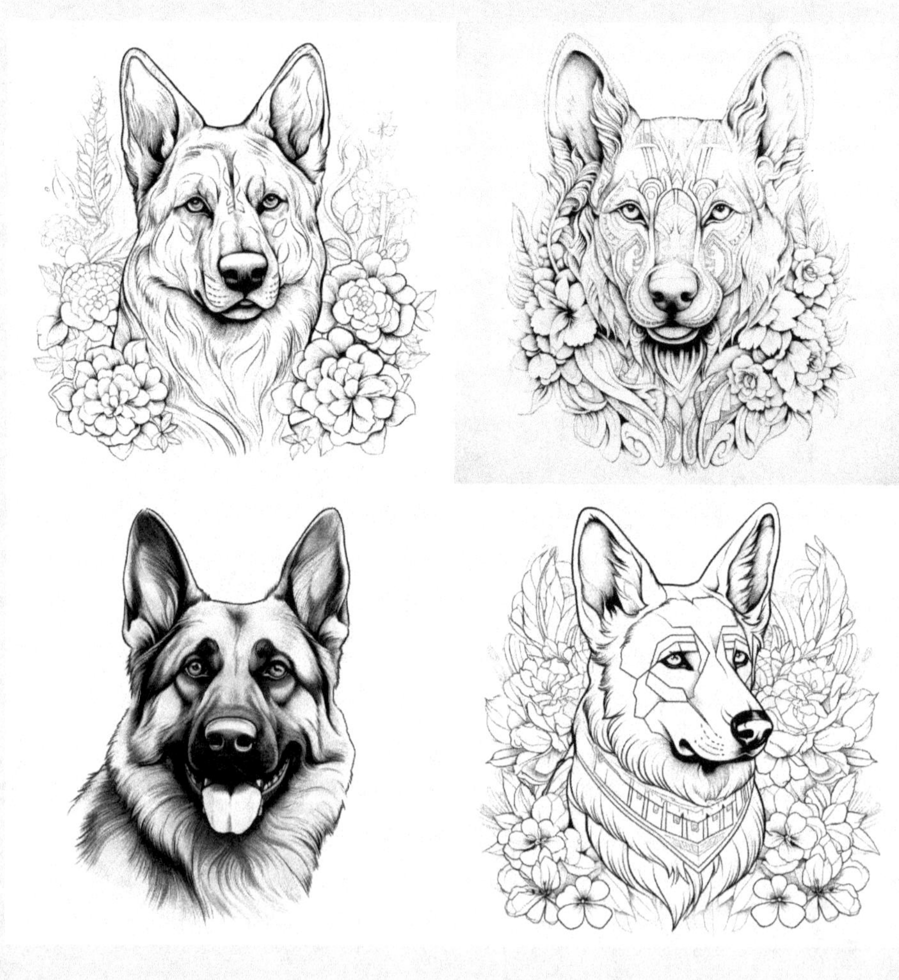

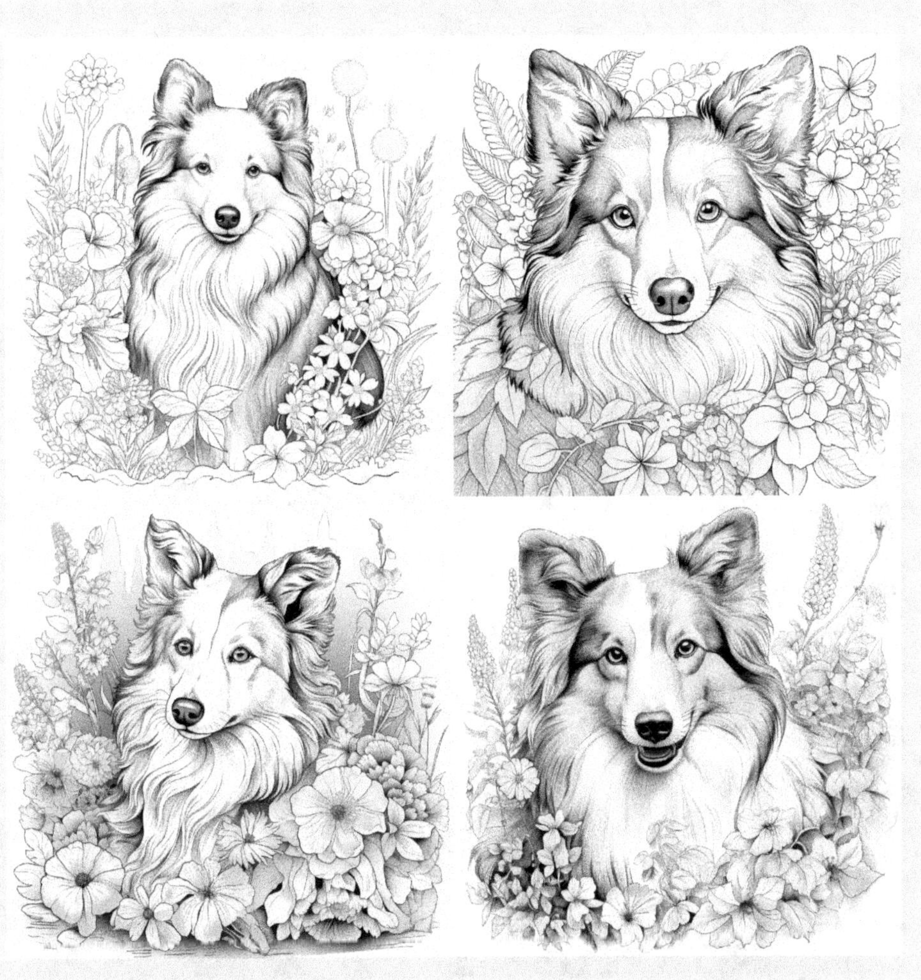

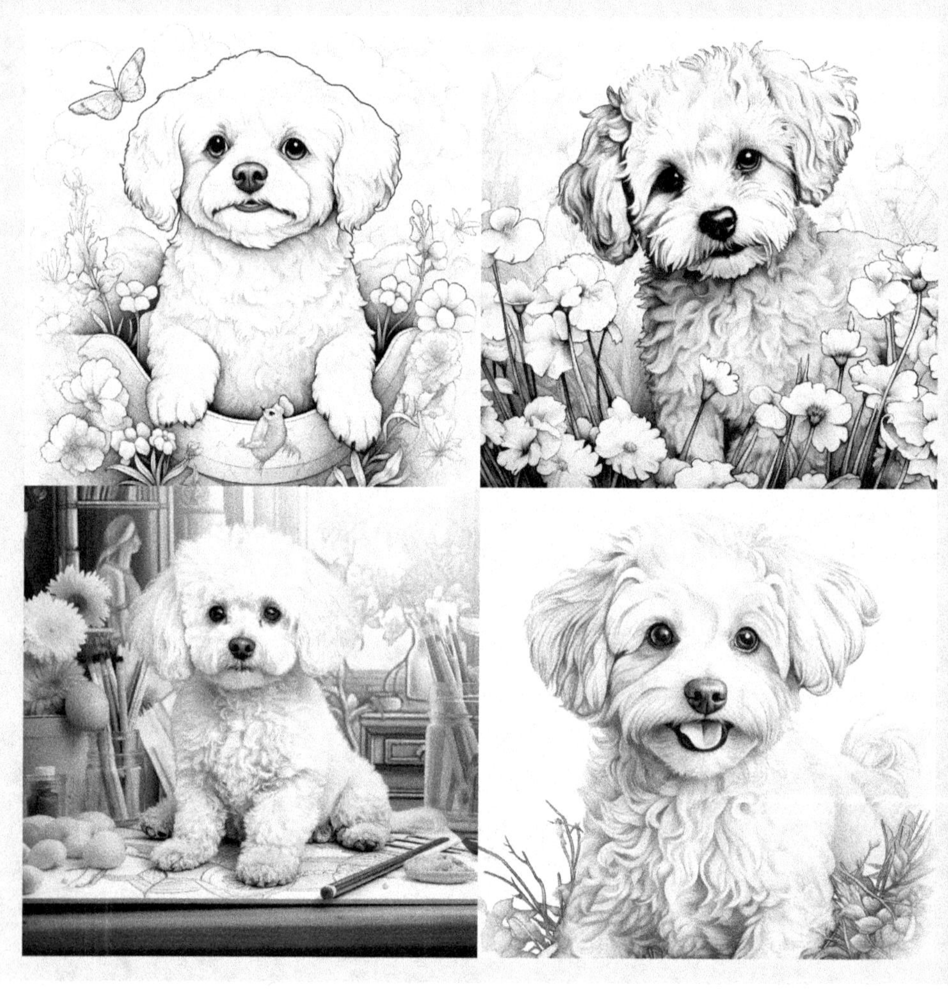

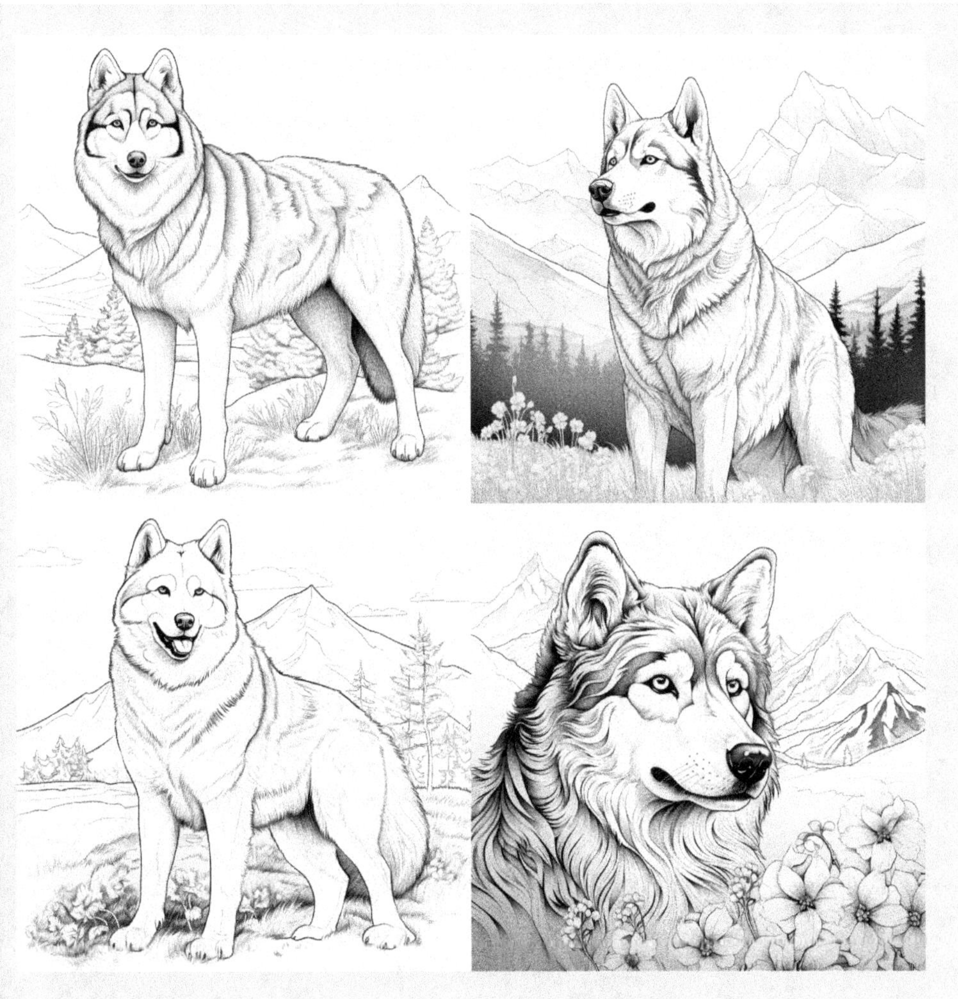

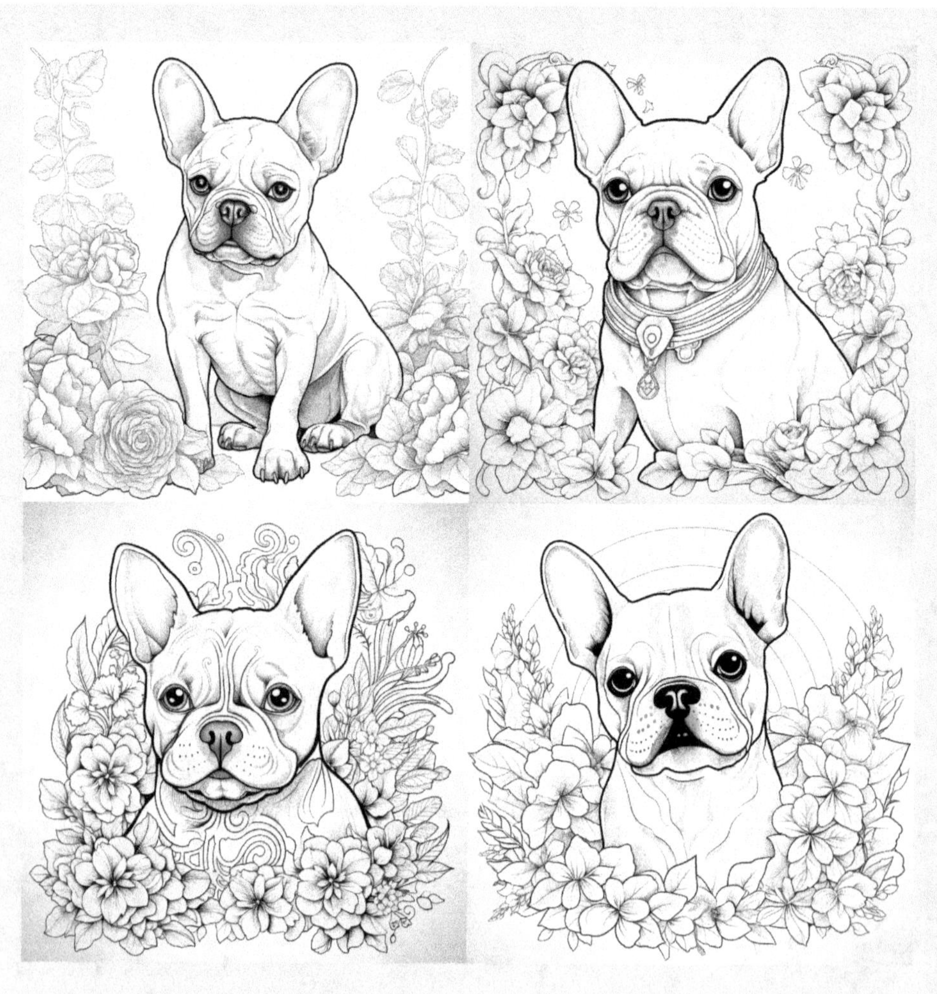

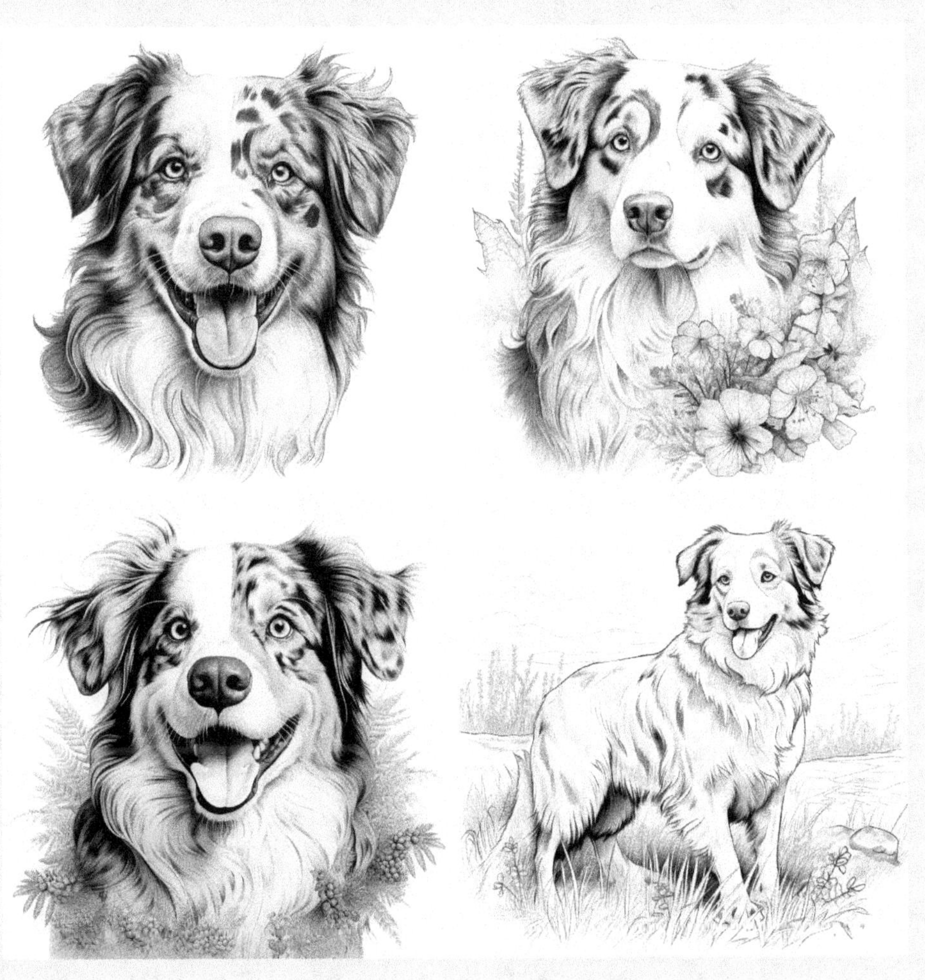

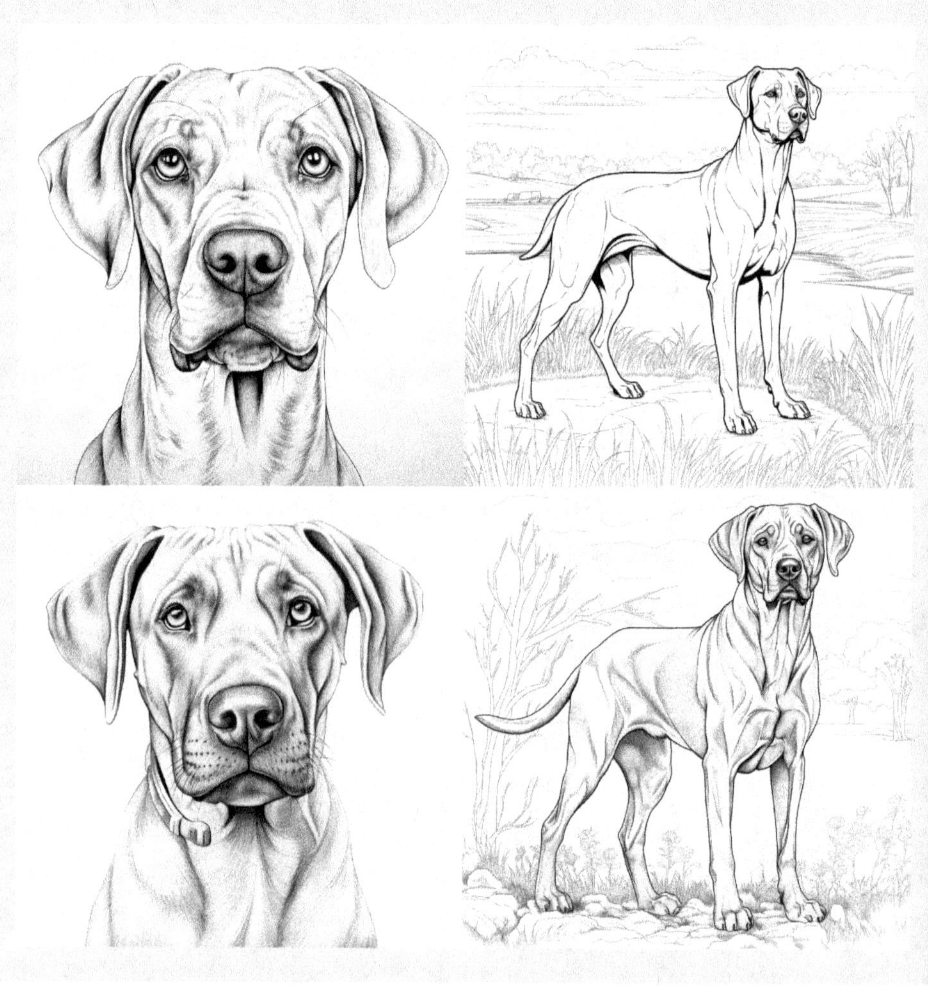

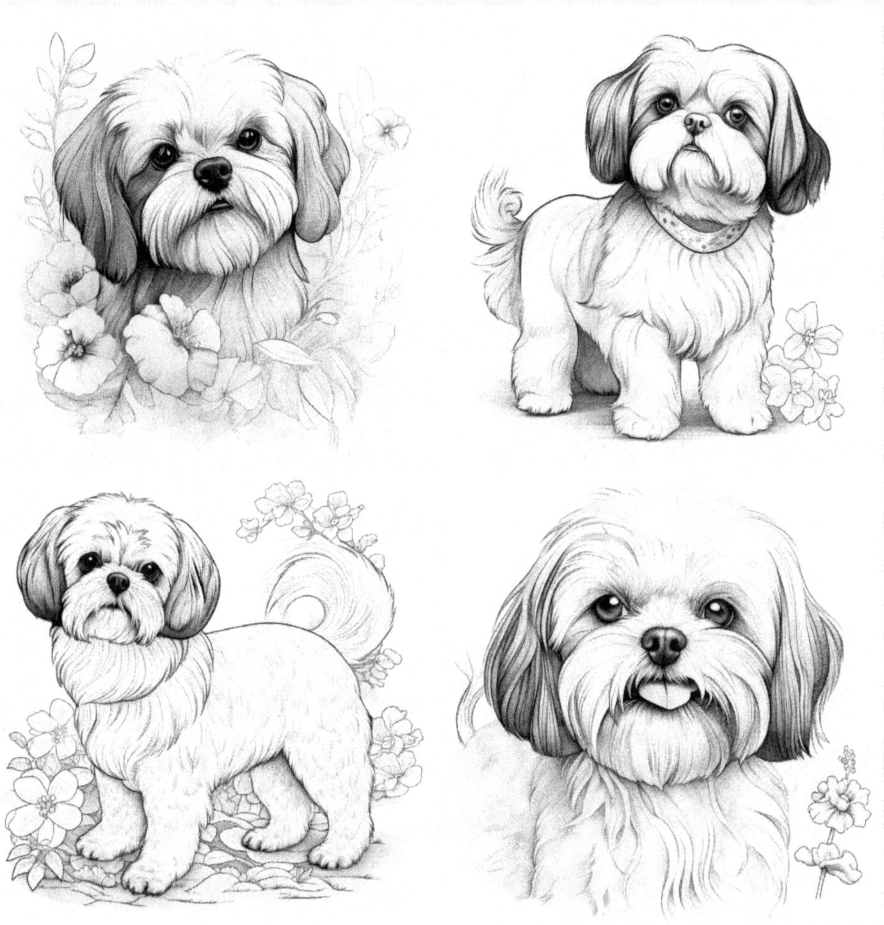

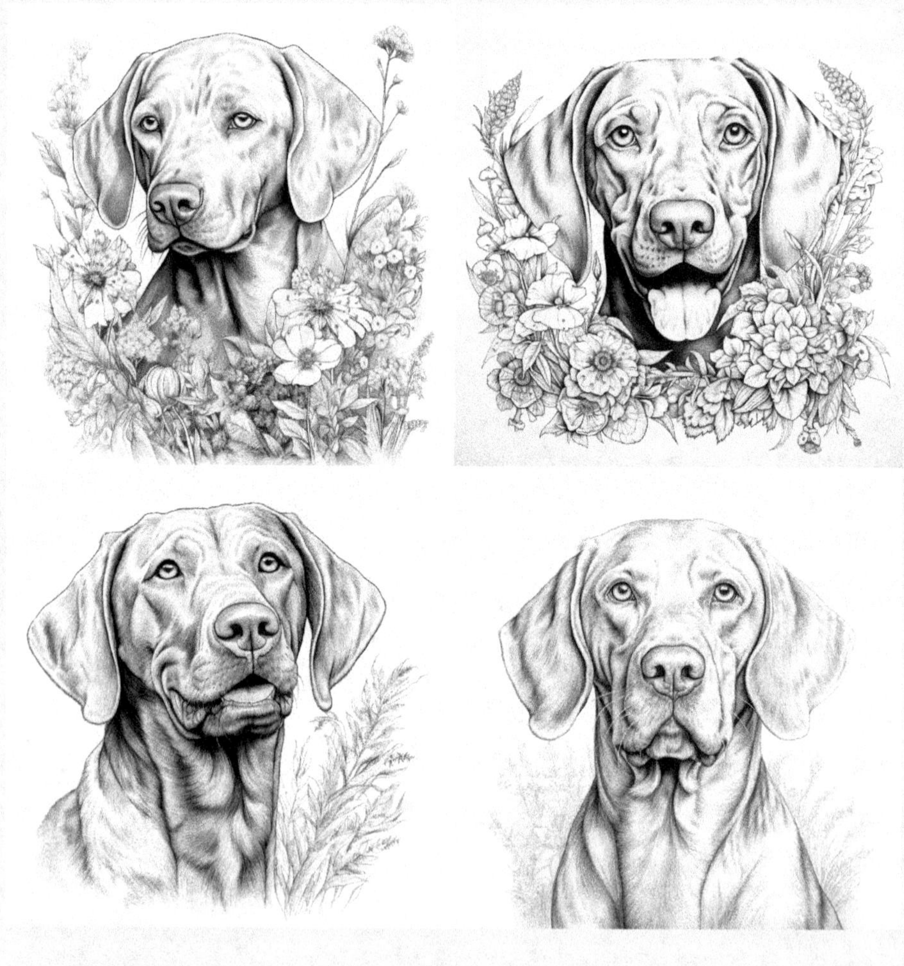

To all dog's lovers

THANK YOU!